What they say about

"I think that your book ... pe-
cially for first year socia... in-
dation for learning. I pa... ess
of the book, which has h... nal
statement. I would defi......... ...ice
once I get onto a social work programme! A great read!
From a student point of view it is a well written book! I understood everything!"

Sophie Dishman, prospective social work student

"Overall, I think the book is an excellent idea. When I started out, I knew I wanted to be a social worker but didn't really know what that meant. I certainly didn't appreciate the number of different roles and functions one could pursue. The book provides very good insight and clarity regarding the opportunities.

It is easy to read – very accessible and gives a good overview of the world of ASC. I would recommend it to my first year students."

Lorna Wallace-Davies, Owner / Director of Change and Development Company, leadership mentor and registered social worker (www.change-develop.com)

"I really, really enjoyed reading the book and found it helpful in working out some ideas for my future. It is unique in consisting of a wide-ranging overview of adult social care with a more personal, mentoring style of guidance. I thoroughly appreciated all the stories of current leaders. I would certainly recommend it to my friends and colleagues."

Sophie Kendall, post-graduate Public Administration student at Green Templeton College, University of Oxford

"I'd recommend the book as practical and positive, appealing to the heart and head. It's personable and informing. The exercises are really useful. They get the reader involved in understanding what making a difference in social care means personally to them, which makes the learning more holistic. It's a possible refresher for people already in social care facing an impasse or redundancy. It helps them think what they want from their career in relation to brain, heart, money, recognition. Lovely!"

Maria Adebowale, Director of Living Space Project, a London leader for fair and greener jobs

Making a Difference in Adult Social Care

Release your leadership ambitions

Richard Pantlin

with cartoons by Fran Orford

℗ Magic Pocket 2014
Revised edition, June 2014
ISBN: 978-1494233365

Copyright © Richard Pantlin 2014
The moral right of the author has been asserted

Graphics by Rita Branco
Cartoons by Fran Orford
Cover by Nathan Shelton
Foreword by Debbie Sorkin
Back cover photo by Robert Taylor

Design and layout by Hafiz Ladell
for Magic Pocket Productions
www.magicpocket.co.uk

Contents

Foreword by Debbie Sorkin	vi
1. Using this book effectively	1
2. Why is Adult Social Care for you?	14
3. Trust your Heart	34
4. How the ASC sector hangs together	40
5. Local political leadership – becoming a Councillor	67
6. You really need to understand Clients and Carers	82
7. "No-one goes into Social Work to become a DASS"	104
8. Your local circle of care	125
9. Making money out of delivering ASC	132
10. Social enterprises & charities – a growing third way	145
11. Big Society and voluntary work	157
12. Policy is worthwhile – Never mind the gap!	162
13. Particular ASC leadership qualities	182
14. Be inspired by existing leaders	206
15. Your roadmap	213
Bibliography	224
Useful websites	225
Index	226

Personal development: the best investment you can make

A foreword from Debbie Sorkin, Chief Executive of the National Skills Academy for Social Care

Social care is one of the largest employers in the country. More than 1.5 million people work in a huge variety of jobs, and Skills for Care have estimated that a million more jobs will be needed in the sector over the next decade, just to keep pace with demographic changes. (See *http://www.skillsforcare.org.uk/Publications "The size and structure of the adult social care workforce 2013"*).

At the same time, social care is becoming more complex, and faces enormous change. So, more than ever, we need a well-trained, well-qualified workforce, composed of people committed to making their careers in care.

Care and support is tremendously demanding work and front-line workers deserve to be well-supported and nurtured; good staff need recognition and developing. They should be celebrated as models of good practice and offered inspiring environments which encourage them to chart career paths and be given lots of positive reasons to stay. One way that employers can reward staff, and encourage them to stay, is by demonstrating their commitment to personal development, so that people see social care as a sector in which they can have a worthwhile career. This book can help with that.

Good leadership is necessary to deliver high quality services to the people who need them. At the Skills Academy we conducted a survey which showed 94% of people in the sector see a clear link. (See *https://www.nsasocialcare.co.uk/about-us/our-publications "Who Cares? Survey 2012"*.)

Good employers are continuing to invest in learning. They see career development as something to invest in from the start.

The key thing is to make time for training and personal development. We know that the main barriers are staff time and costs. Employers can overcome these in three ways:

1) Use on-site learning or blended approaches that include online training, reducing staff travel time and the need to back-fill posts.

2) A way to reduce costs is to offer spare places on your courses to neighbouring care organisations, especially smaller ones – perhaps in return for training in other areas, or for providing cover while your staff undertake learning and development.

3) An alternative approach is shadowing and coaching. We know from our own experience that coaching approaches which encourage self-reflection are a recognised way to sustain and build continuous improvement. This book offers some great exercises for practising self-reflection.

In the end, the best argument for leadership development is this: If you invest in yourself and your organisation, you can transform the quality of the service you provide. So wherever you are in Social Care – whether you're a Care Assistant, a Manager, or working at senior level – if you want to stand out and you want your service to excel, invest in your career and development. It's the best investment you will ever make.

Chapter One

Using this book effectively

OK, you've made a good start here at Chapter One. It's worth reading this chapter first and in full – just like when you unpack a new board game, it's a good idea to first read the instructions before you start playing. It may be you are reading this as an e-book. It doesn't make much difference in how you use it.

But, if you have shelled out on the hard copy, then you do have one advantage: **you can write all over it!**

And you can ear-mark the pages, too. I wouldn't want to see a pristine copy of this book sitting on your shelf in 6 months' time – regardless of whether you have read it or not. I *do* want to meet you in 5 or 15 years' time and hear you say that this book gave you some great ideas that have helped you really make a difference in your chosen field of adult social care!

(For e-book readers: you can always write out points of value using old-fashioned pen and paper and stick them on your wall with Blu Tack.)

Whether you are writing on a hard copy or copying out ideas, **use colours!**

I will come back to that point.

Here comes the next tip:

You don't have to read Chapter Two next and then go on to Chapter Three!

Yes, I've put the chapters in a sequence that makes sense to me. No doubt you will have your own interests and priorities. In a moment, I'll give you an exercise to explore these.

These days we are being constantly bombarded with information. We can gain access to a large part of the world's knowledge with a simple click of the mouse or a couple of taps on a smartphone screen. This was the vision that inspired the founders of Google, and within less than 15 years we have come close to achieving it. I still find that quite incredible. We are still exploring the effects of this new global connectedness. Who knows where it will have taken us after a further 15 years?

Of course, one big question is whether all this makes us happier as human beings. It has certainly brought new pressures. We are open to all sorts of communications from hundreds more people than ever before – and they all come with some kind of emotional baggage attached. Some communications are easily dismissed – here's yet another spam email promoting Viagra! But even then, just for a fraction of a second, don't certain thoughts flit through your mind, such as: 'Who sends these?... Why?... Who responds?... And, actually, isn't my (or my boyfriend's) erectile capability good enough?'

You may be getting impatient now and wondering what this has to do with making a career in adult social care. Well, actually it does. We will come on to that later.

Just for now, enjoy reading this quickly and feel free to skim where you need to.

Let me continue with my theme for a moment.

Other communications may have a bigger impact. For example, if you've noticed that the Kony 2012 video on YouTube has received 83 million hits, you may, having spent 29 minutes watching it, feel obliged to spend another half an hour checking how other people have responded – because surely if 83 million people think it's worth watching, it must be significant, mustn't it, and you wouldn't want to feel left out, would you?

And so you might not only find out about an African warlord who has kidnapped children to be soldiers in his 'crusade'. As you investigate the comments left by viewers, you may also notice that many people are taking offence at how the film-maker – some white American – is demonising the warlord. If this moves you to engage in some action to improve the world, then all well and good. But too often we are left feeling confused and powerless, overwhelmed and frustrated with all this information – and its emotional content.

The key skill that a baby's brain learns in order for it to survive is the ability to filter out the vast majority of sensory perceptions coming through its eyes, ears, nose, mouth and skin. As a society we are still learning how best to filter the new, mainly visual, communication channels and how to respond, or not, to their emotional content. Friends are important to all of us – but if you have 500 'friends' on Facebook, how many should you keep up with as 'best friends'? Should you comment on their every status update – and should you do so for all to see, or send a private message?

My point is that the following factors are relevant not only to how you use this book, but also to how you go about caring for vulnerable adults:

- ✶ Your relationships with friends and family
- ✶ Your degree of emotional connectedness
- ✶ How you go about prioritising communications
- ✶ The particular things that make you happy
- ✶ The extent to which you feel empowered / disempowered.

Your time – all our time – is short and valuable.

One of the consequences of the huge expansion in our communication networks is the sense that we have much less time than we would like.

We also have less time because we increasingly feel we have to earn the money to keep up with everyone else – unless you are lucky enough to be in the top 1% of the wealthy in the world!

It may just be a matter of taking on that Saturday job while you are studying so you can afford the mobile airtime you need to keep up with your friends, or it may mean keeping your boss happy by working nine-hour days, plus commuting an hour each way, all in order to earn the salary that maintains your house and family.

The fact is, time spent reading this book is time when you **won't be** earning money, enjoying the company of friends and family, engaging in study or indulging in your hobby.

That's why I've made it quick and easy to read – interesting and fun, I hope! – and also why I'd like to give you a couple more tips on how to use it most effectively.

I estimate that you should spend no more than 5 to 14 hours reading this book, including doing the exercises. It depends on how fast you read and whether you are interested in all of it or just want to pick and choose.

Either way, it amounts to a good investment if it can help you just a little to make more effective use of the next 10 to 15 years of your life.

You have bought this book – or been given it if you are lucky! – because you are starting, or have been thinking about, a career in adult social care. I am going to help you consider why you might want to embark on such a career – why it may indeed be ideally suited to you. I will explore career options and paths that you might not have thought about. I hope I will be able to inspire you to make a difference in the sector. Over the last five years it has been going through enormous changes, and this is sure to continue as the population ages, and as we undergo the various demographic shifts affecting England and the rest of the world. These are challenges that we need people like you to help with!

Getting down to making the most of this book, here's a fun

Using this book effectively

exercise to get you started.

I'm sure you'll have noticed the various symbols at the start of this and other chapters.

I've used four:

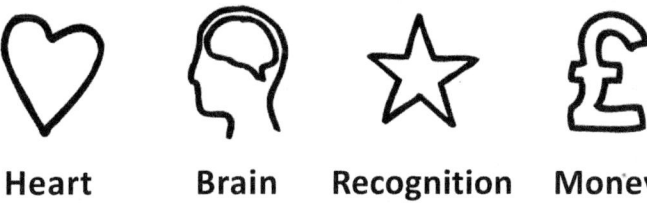

Heart   **Brain**   **Recognition**   **Money**

These represent four different aspects of careers. Each one of us will be motivated by different combinations of those four factors – and this mix will no doubt change over time as well. The symbols appear throughout the book to indicate particular aspects under consideration.

On the next page, you will see these symbols as headings above empty columns.

Please take a pen or pencil – or even better, coloured crayons or felt tip pens – and draw more of those symbols under each column.

If you are using colours, then these are the ones that work for me:

Heart – red or pink   **Money** – black or brown

Brain – blue or green   **Recognition** – yellow or orange

You could start by colouring in the printed symbols.

Then, thinking about what you want from life and what the symbols mean to you, draw more symbols under the column(s) that are most important to you. Act on impulse without analysing it yet.

Don't worry about accuracy. An oval scribble with a nose for the head / brain will do. You should be able to manage the star in five continuous strokes – it gets easier with practice!

Making a Difference in Adult Social Care

Exercise One

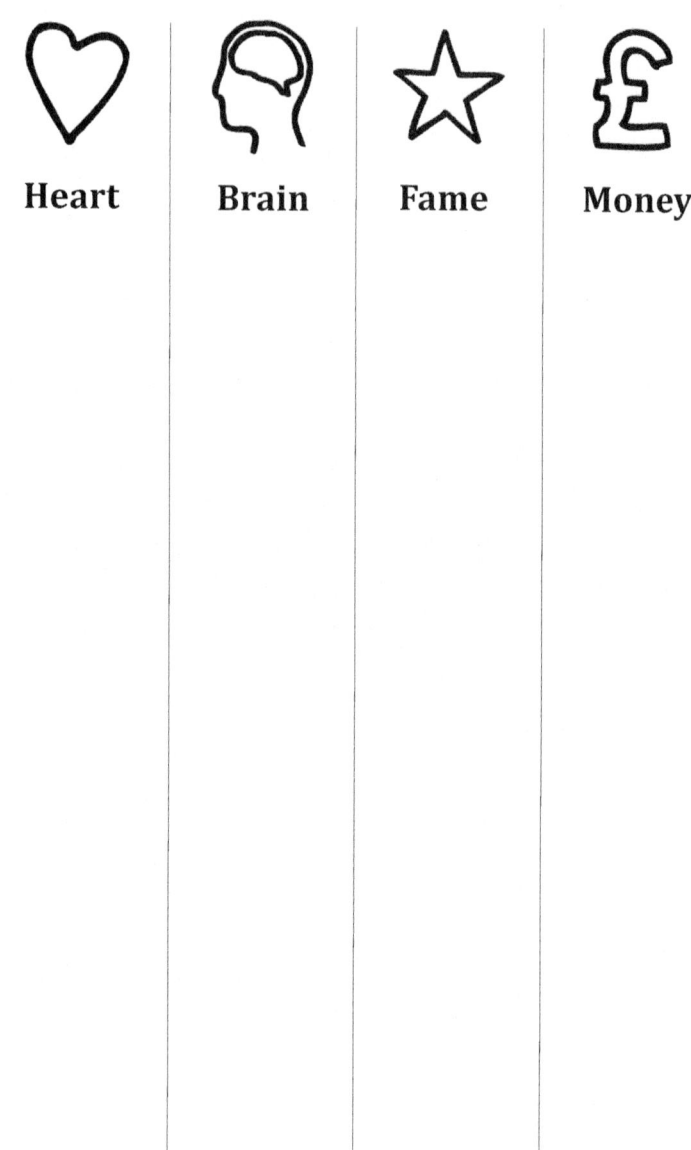

Heart	Brain	Fame	Money

Using this book effectively

How many of each seem right for you? Draw them in.

If you really don't want to draw the symbols, then just mark a tally.

OK, happy with that?

Now you can use your rational left brain to think about what this says about you.

If you have more hearts than you have stars, then it suggests that you are more interested in building warm, close personal relationships and caring than you are in making a name for yourself and achieving public recognition.

If you have more pound signs than brain symbols, it could just be that they are easier to draw – we are after all only too familiar with pound signs! On the other hand, it may be an indication that you are more interested in making money out of a career than in the intellectual challenges that it might present.

Count the number of symbols you have drawn in each column and write that number under your column of symbols. You may feel uncomfortable with the result – don't worry, there'll be a chance to change it in a moment, and you don't have to show anyone!

So, let's explore the significance of the symbols some more, as we will be making use of them throughout the book.

Heart

This represents the emotions. It's about human relationships, caring, friends and family.

Naturally, it lies at the 'heart' or centre of social care as a vocation, but don't worry if you have scored yourself relatively low under this heading. There are many reasons why you might be going into a job or career in social care. Right now, maybe it's the only means you can identify of earning a living. Well, there might well be a reason why a caring job or study subject has presented itself as an option just now rather than, say, working in a shop or studying engineering.

Money

We all know what this means, don't we?

It might seem to you that there is a direct conflict between Heart and Money, as if there is a crucial choice to be made between the two. Well, yes, I've just asked you to make choices, and you will inevitably have to face such choices in your career, but, nonetheless, **the two needn't be mutually exclusive.** One of the things that I wish to demonstrate, by drawing on real life examples, is that you can be a caring person and offer great care while still making a very good living for yourself and your family. There is certainly no shame in that. Many of the most successful entrepreneurs would agree with the proposition that due rewards are sure to come your way, as long as you put yourself in service to others.

Now, rewards may take other forms than the merely financial, which brings us onto the next symbol.

Recognition

The star represents public recognition. If your circle of recognition is a wide one, this might correspond to fame, or celebrity. It might arise from being the head of a large organisation, with hundreds of people knowing your face and your name, even if they don't really know you as a person. It might be a consequence of your putting yourself in the public eye as a public speaker, campaigner, or political activist.

Or it could just be that you are known and respected by your local group of colleagues, clients and peers.

Public recognition needn't involve constantly having your face and name in the papers. It may simply mean that there is a group of people who know and respect you for the difference that you make in their lives or the lives of people they care for. They may not tell you to your face how much they value your contribution, but they will probably tell their friends.

Lastly,

Brain

This represents the pleasure that many of us derive from grappling with, and solving, difficult problems.

Over the years many of the people I've spoken to about their workplace and job have told me that what they appreciate most is the stimulation of working with other intelligent people. I don't mean that what is represented by this symbol applies only to people who can score highly in an IQ test. IQ tests measure only one sort of intelligence, but there are various other forms of intelligence to which we all have access, to a greater or lesser extent. Collectively, they form the wisdom of our species. Some people are indeed gifted with facility in solving the mathematical and verbal quizzes measured in IQ tests. Others are particularly blessed with Emotional Intelligence (also known as EQ), an empathic understanding which enables them to interact more effectively with other people, to win them over, gain their trust, or at least lend a sympathetic ear.

I would also like to mention other forms of intelligence. For example, there's something we might call Spiritual Intelligence (SQ), which enables the possessor to be in touch with what really matters in this world, to be contemplative, to be unafraid of the big issues of birth, life and death. Sometimes people with a very strong SQ might seem other-worldly or a little absent, but at times of crisis they can be a godsend – and in adult social care there will be many crises to be dealt with.

A fourth form of intelligence might also be identified, which I will call Physical Intelligence or PQ. People with a high PQ are often busy and their response to a problem is most likely to be to spring into action. It is almost as if their bodies will register what needs to be done and then impel them to just do it. They may have a tendency to get impatient with people who want to analyse first, check other people's feelings or pray / meditate for guidance. But as long as they are in touch at some level with their purpose, then their interventions can be second to none.

To return to the Brain symbol, it is about relishing challenges, confident that your particular range of intelligences will be able address them. It is also about enjoying the company of, or at least having access to, other people with a similar motivation.

Now that I have explained these symbols, let's take another look at how important each one is to you. Then, if you want to, you can skip to those particular sections of the book which feature the symbols that inspire or interest you the most.

Exercise Two

1) Write the tally of symbols from the last exercise. Perhaps your scoresheet looks something like this:-

Heart	Brain	Fame	Money
4	0	2	3

Maybe you weren't sure what the brain / head represented,

Using this book effectively

so you put a couple of stars down because you always liked getting them from your teacher when you were in school . . .

2) Now you've thought more about what the symbols mean, you can make a new tally – a 'gut update', without thinking too much about it – as to which factors are most important for you in your career.

3) Finally, now's the time to engage your logical left brain. Think about how your career might develop over the next 5 to 15 years. Make a rational and realistic assessment of which of our four factors are likely to motivate you. Which fit best with how you define yourself and your personality? Which will also support the other significant things in your life, such as family or hobbies? You may wish to increase or decrease any or all of your symbols. Bear in mind that the higher the scores, the more you will be committing yourself to your future in adult social care.

You may decide that one or more of these aspects could be satisfied outside of your career. Remember, though, you'll need to allow yourself enough time and energy for this.

Distribute at least 15 points across the four columns.

Write the numbers in bigger digits at the bottom of the columns.

Score	Heart	Brain	Fame	Money
Original				
Gut update				
Realistic target				

These numbers represent your current objectives in terms of what you want to gain out of working in adult care.

This can form a guide as to how you use this book. So, if you have lots of Stars, you may wish to pick out the chapters headed with Stars.

But bear in mind that symbols of each type are hidden within each chapter. You'll be able to collect a mix as you go through, and you might be surprised by some you come across. I can't guarantee an equal spread of symbols being available throughout the book – life is not like that, and especially not adult care.

If you have those coloured pens or crayons that I recommended earlier and a spare ten minutes, then I suggest you amuse yourself now by skimming through the book and colouring in the symbols where you find them. Go on, give it a try – even if just for two minutes. Be like a toddler – but neater, please! Show my book some respect!

The inspiration for using symbols like this comes from a board game that I used to play a lot with my family when I was a child. It was called 'Careers'. At the outset you have to set yourself a secret target of the mix of Happiness, Money and Fame that you aim to achieve in your career, i.e. during the course of the game. This target needs to total 60 points, however you choose to distribute them. You then throw dice to progress around the board, choosing different paths representing different study and career options. So if you choose the Business path, this will improve your financial prospects. If Lunar Exploration is your career of choice (yes, I grew up in the 1960's!) then this will greatly increase your Fame points, albeit at the risk of losing all your Happiness if you land on the wrong square. You can also 'buy' Happiness points, signified by being able to buy a yacht! Well, I suppose it works for some people.

In the board game, you keep your target secret. In real life, you don't have to do that but you may wish to be circumspect as to whom you share it with. By the end of this book you may wish to revise your targets – or perhaps set one target for the next three years, then expect to focus on a different factor for the following five. In any case, I have included an exercise at the end of the book for considering different time perspectives.

Final thoughts on using this book effectively

Allow yourself the luxury of some uninterrupted time and space. I want you to be able to contemplate and digest what you've been reading – not just to scan the words on the page and allow them to fall straight out of your head again.

Even if you can only manage a 15 minute session, try turning off your mobile phone for that time. (No friend, colleague or manager should expect a response in less time than that unless they have made a specific arrangement for you to be on call.)

If possible, find a room where you can work without interruption or distraction. Have a pen and coloured pencils to hand, ready to catch your thoughts. You already have my permission to write on the hard copy book, or you could keep another notepad you can refer back to. Perhaps you prefer to cover your wall with post-it notes!

Tell your partner / friends / family that you are going to focus on something important regarding your future and you don't want to be interrupted for a specified period. Naturally, it's best not to be hung-over or intoxicated in any way. You may want to try a short burst of exercise or get some fresh air before each session, so your energy is running freely.

My recommendation is to set aside an hour or so, two or three times a week until you are finished. This should be easily achievable, however busy you are. Between sessions, as you go about the rest of your current daily life, including those activities already related to caring for adults, you will have the opportunity to absorb and reflect upon the insights that you are receiving.

Chapter Two

Why is Adult Social Care for you?

It helps to know why you are interested in adult social care, so let's explore this.

It may be obvious to you.

Perhaps you were looking for work and someone suggested you might be interested in this job in adult social care (ASC), so you just said: "OK, I'll give it a go." And here you are a month or a year or two years later.

Perhaps, like Terry Dafter, a Director of Adult Social Services whom we will meet later, you have studied something generic like Sociology and your tutor has suggested progressing on to a vocational course, gaining a social work qualification which could lead to employment.

Maybe social work appeals to you because you just want to help people, and it doesn't really matter to you whether it involves working with children or adults.

We'll come to the differences between adult social work and working with children soon, but first let's explore a little deeper as to why you think adult social care might be a fulfilling career for you. Then we'll come on to what you might gain from it and also briefly discuss some of the pressures that you will have to face and deal with.

You may feel that your entering a career in social care was a rather random decision – perhaps you were simply following someone's suggestion. Bear in mind that such impulses come from somewhere. It's quite likely that something about you – your caring nature, your general aptitude, your personal history – provoked that suggestion. If it was your own idea, however unclearly defined, acknowledge that there was something about social care that just appealed to you and connected with your life experience.

Again this might be clear and straightforward to you and you might wish to skim forward through this section. You may, for example, have been inspired by a social worker that you have known.

Perhaps you yourself had to deal with the sort of situation in which social care can help. Terry Dafter, for example, grew up with a mother suffering from what we would now call bi-polar condition. Her mental health problems meant that sometimes he would come home from school to find that she had spent all day sitting crying in the darkened back room. Then there would be other days when the windows and doors would be open, music would be playing, and she would be on a high.

Perhaps like Rita, of whom we hear more later, you have one or more grandparents with dementia and want to find out what can be done to help them, and people like them, in their old age.

Perhaps someone you know has been running a care home for people with Down's Syndrome and you admire the work they do, the patience they show and the difference they make to their clients.

Now, even if you think you are clear why you are involved in adult care, I'd like you to take a few minutes to close your eyes and meditate on the factors that have led you to consider this area of work.

Use the blank space on the next page to jot down what comes to mind: experiences, particular times in your life, people's names. If you get images appearing in your mind, scribble them down.

Each time you've written a few things, go back to closing your eyes and pondering.

OK, once you've finished letting thoughts and memories flow, go back over the page and draw a circle round, or highlight with a colour, those items you find most significant.

Think about what stands out and write down your ideas.

In future years, when you're reflecting back on the choices you made and wondering if you made the right call, you may well find it useful to have this record. Also, if people ask you why you are in social care, you will have the answer – though how much of it you wish to share will of course depend on how personal it is and how much you trust the other person. Remember, trust in someone can often engender reciprocal trust.

Children's social work or adult social care?

When the members of the general public think of a social worker, they normally have in mind someone who is trying to help difficult children or who is trying to protect a very young child from incompetent and dangerous parents. I'm aware that this sentence may not sound 'politically correct', because we shouldn't really be talking about children being 'difficult' or parents being judged as 'incompetent', at risk of their children being taken away, but I simply wish to portray a common way of thinking. I don't propose in this book to go into the whys and wherefores of that language. Suffice to say that 'social work' is normally associated first and foremost with children.

And it may indeed be what first attracted you to social work. After all, children are vulnerable and innocent and need to be helped and protected if they are at risk. (Well, yes and no, and no and yes, actually ... but, again, that is for another book.)

Now, I'm talking here about being a social worker, but let me emphasise that this book is not just for people wanting to become qualified social workers. Adult social care is a far wider field than that, and a degree in social work is not essential in order to make a difference.

In England there has even been some debate as to whether academically qualified social workers are at all needed in adult care. Even before the Coalition Government's latest austerity programme, many local authorities (LAs) have been saving money by filling positions previously held by social workers with other less qualified staff, on reduced salaries. For example, all assessments of need used to be carried out by qualified social workers, which, in general, was not only expensive but led to long delays in care delivery. Consequently, over the last ten years most authorities have introduced initial assessments that can be carried out by staff who are not qualified social workers, but whose training and experience may have stemmed from having previously been in an administrative support role. In more complex situations a properly qualified social worker may still be required to complete a full assessment. In some cases, this will be done by an Occupational Therapist (OT) or even by both together.

It also used to be the case that adult social care workers would arrange the package of care for the client deemed eligible for LA support. Twenty years ago, most of that support was provided by LA staff or residential homes and was straightforward to arrange within the public sector. The downside was that it tended to be inflexible, sometimes of poor quality (or at least lacking in choice) and questionable value for money. Nowadays most support is delivered by the private sector or the not-for-profit sector. This does mean that there is more complexity in arranging contracts – especially if the care is for some reason unusual and doesn't fit under an existing LA 'block contract' with a provider (where these still exist). 'Brokering' a package of care, often from a combination of different providers, could easily consume a lot of time: checking availability, completing the paperwork, calculating costs against available spending limits, etc. Many LAs considered this to be not the best use of qualified social workers' time and therefore introduced the new roles of 'care manager' or 'support broker': people who could step in after a qualified social worker had assessed the general needs that were required to be met by the package of care. It is also true that social workers were not trained for this contracting role and were often not very interested in it. In the last few years 'Personalisation' has taken this a step further, so that it is up to clients or their carers to make these arrangements themselves.

One consequence of these changes over the last two decades is that, in England, we tend to talk about adult social care rather than adult social work. This has been particularly the case following the division of responsibilities between the Director of Adult Social Services (DASS) and the Director of Children's Services (including child protection) that was introduced in 2006. This does not apply to Scotland and Wales, where social work departments are still responsible for both adults and children. Also, in Scotland they include the equivalent of Youth Justice and the Probation Service, which in England are organised differently.

When you completed the exercise on what attracted you to social care, you might have identified many factors relating to children. You may still be wondering which is for you: children's social work or adult social care. Let's consider some simple similarities and differences.

At the risk of stating the bleeding obvious, they are both about caring and supporting people through difficult times. They often involve very personal emotional issues and need to take into account a wide range of factors and individuals beyond the immediate 'client'.

In some respects, dealing with very vulnerable adults may be a little like dealing with children. We all retain many of the emotional patterns that we formed as children, although we may have become skilful in handling or masking them. Just like children, adults can need protection and safeguarding – and, yes, just as in children's social work this can sometimes mean confronting others around them who are seen to be failing in their duty of care.

A large proportion of LA adult social care is for people with Learning Disabilities (LD). It would be a gross over-simplification to say that people with LD behave rather like children, but there is nonetheless some truth in this.

On the other hand, social care is not primarily about helping people in the sense of you deciding what is best for them and then ensuring that this is delivered. Even 30 years ago that was not the nature of good social work, and 'personalisation' has made this less true than ever, as regards working with both adults and children.

Personalisation means that, as a good social worker, you always have to listen carefully to the client, whether adult or child, to determine their circumstances, find out what is important to them and then offer advice as to how they can best improve their own lives in the context of their available support networks, whilst taking into account the various pressures they are under.

Nevertheless, there are differences. You might be attracted to working with children because of their innocence, their cuteness. Of course, the older children get and the more they need social services intervention, so may these qualities diminish. What is certainly true is that children are more pliable, and a small change in their circumstances now is quite likely to have a significant impact for many years to come. A decisive intervention or sustained support over just a few months could reverberate over an entire lifetime, to the benefit of both the child and society as a whole.

In children's social care, whether it be as as a social worker, a family support worker, a foster carer or a member of staff in a residential home, you are likely to have a longer and more

Why is Adult Social Care for you?

in-depth involvement with your 'client'. You will also have to engage with a range of family members and their friends. This may also be true in adult social care, though generally to a lesser extent, particularly as regards the largest 'client group', the elderly. You will tend to have a shorter, more superficial engagement with the client (unless you are working in a residential home) and even then, many older people will keep to themselves or else be so frail that little interaction is possible.

It is a little different when engaging with people with Learning Disabilities, which may involve a longer ongoing relationship and abundant communication. In all cases, the objective is to encourage the person to live as independently as possible.

In adult social care, you need always to remember that the people you are working with have a long backstory – sometimes much longer than your whole life. Their life experience is likely to have been very different to yours. Growing up in different times and places will have engendered a system of values which you may find challenging. It is your job to support them, so you will have to tolerate and, if possible, respect their views – however diametrically opposed they might be to yours.

Of course, there might still be occasions where you simply have to say that you cannot work with a certain individual – which might be better for both of you. An obvious example might be the constant aggravation encountered by a black  woman carer working with an elderly white man of implacable and deeply racist beliefs, being obliged to provide intimate personal care on a day-to-day basis. These situations do arise and have to be managed.

In general, though, as Meg Barbour, a voluntary organiser and carers' representative, said to me:

> *"A social worker has to work alongside whoever has a problem – to support them, sometimes to make suggestions but in no way to tell them what to do.*

A social worker has to be completely unbiased, without any prejudice. Although they may feel horror inside at what a person has done, it must not show."

What are the paybacks from working in Adult Social Care?

Let's go through them in general terms. Other chapters will focus on various aspects of work in the social care sector and how they have their own balance of rewards: emotional, financial, intellectual challenge, etc.

Heart

Number one has to be the satisfaction that you get when you help to improve someone's life. Everyone's heart swells up a little if they feel they've made another person's life better. I'm sure you wouldn't be reading this book if this was not important to you.

Of course, that's not to say that every hour of every day in adult social care will feel like you are bringing rays of sunshine to those around you. There is a lot of bureaucracy, form-filling and routine in ASC. Sometimes there is a good reason for this: we will touch on that in the chapter on being a Director of Adult Social Services (DASS).

Also, quite frankly, you may have some clients that you feel very little warmth towards. You might find that most of your clients are unappreciative and grumbly.

Even if they do value your help and hard work, they might never tell you.

You will need to have a strong core of your own self-belief and certainty in what you are doing. As Meg Barbour describes:

"When I am interviewing a prospective social worker, what I look for is someone who has got themselves together. That's terribly important. Unless you have a very firm hold on yourself, your self-esteem and your own ideas, you can't help others – it has to be that way. I interview kids sometimes who are 17 or 18 and they say they just want to help. What we tell them is to go away and get some experience.

Sometimes young people want to enter care work because they have been in care or been adopted or had experience of a good social worker coming in their own home for a brother or sister. Or sometimes they just want to help and that is lovely, but when we hear that we go 'oh dear', because it's not quite so easy as that. You have to be very strong emotionally. What you are going to hear is going to challenge everything inside you. You have to take it all in and somehow process it and live your life outside it and not be affected."

This book is about really making a difference – not just to a limited number of direct clients, but in the wider field of social care, becoming in due course a leader, someone whom your peers respect. This brings us on to the second payback:

Public recognition

This might be just a matter of a fairly small number of local people being aware of what you do and knowing it to be a good thing (without even really talking about it).

This reminds me of when I was in my early twenties.

It was a time – the early Thatcher years – of high unemployment. After graduation, finding it hard to get a job myself, I helped set up the Oxford Unemployed Workers & Claimants Union. It was dedicated to empowering people who were unemployed or claiming other benefits. We helped each other with benefit claims, appeals and tribunals. We also campaigned for better arrangements and against the media depiction of people like us as 'scroungers'. We obtained enough funding from the city council for a half-time employee and I was given that job when the first person moved on.

Nowadays, we might call the operation a Social Enterprise or claim to be part of the Big Society but in those days we were motivated by socialist ideals and looked back to Unemployed Workers' struggles during the Great Depression of the late twenties and thirties.

Anyway, although I was at first scraping along on social security, and subsequently living barely above that level, I gained great satisfaction from a degree of local public recognition for the work that I did. It was great to have people nod and smile at me as I did my shopping in the local Tesco's. Sometimes they might know my name even though I didn't know or remember theirs.

Public recognition can be important to all of us, even on a small local scale.

 **Brain**

Mental and intellectual challenges abound in adult social care – particularly as you move into any kind of leadership role.

You will need to deploy the whole range of intelligences we discussed earlier – rational, emotional, physical and spiritual – and you will gain the consequent satisfaction of using these skills to overcome all manner of obstacles – your internal self-doubts, external hindrances, and your clients' resistance. This overlaps with the **Heart** satisfaction that is available to you in adult social care, so let's focus more on the rational challenges and rewards.

You may not think of yourself as intellectual or particularly good at mental problem-solving: this may have been the mark of a geek when you were at school. But you may nonetheless find strengths in this department that you have undervalued.

Certainly for Terry Dafter, the Director of Adult Social Services at Stockport council, the mental challenges were a key reason why he kept progressing through the ranks from Team Leader, Area Manager, Assistant Director, all the way to the top. If you show some aptitude in organisational ability and are lucky enough to have a good manager or mentor, then you will be encouraged to take on bigger jobs. The payback comes from seeing how you can grasp increasingly complex situations involving more and more people. Then you can develop systems and processes for managing them and learn to deliver better outcomes for clients and staff.

Such experiences of personal development can be highly satisfying.

It also tends to be true that the more you move into a leadership role, the more you are mixing with an immediate set of peers who are motivated by similar intelligences – itself a source of satisfaction.

There is another way in which you can achieve **Brain** payback in adult social care, and that is by moving into the field of policy and/or academia. I am lumping these together because good policy needs to be underpinned by good academic work. The two fields overlap in the area of think tanks. A prime example in adult social care is the King's Fund, and there are a range of others including Demos. These organisations employ people who carry out original research and assess other more academic material in order to come up with policy recommendations for government. A number of charities and pressure groups like Age UK and MIND play a similar role, in addition to their practical 'ground-level' work supporting a wide range of local projects and groups.

It's their job to work out precisely how things work, through designing statistical surveys, then carefully analysing the results and drawing the appropriate conclusions, in order to inform how adult social care is delivered in the future. As I said, think tanks sit in the middle of this space, with "pure" academic research on one hand and policy writing for ministers (or on a smaller scale for DASS's and Councillors) on the other. The latter tends to be strongly concerned with presentation and in assessing what will be acceptable to the general public. Just finding the right words and phrases to describe changes in policy can at times seem as important as the actual policy itself. However, pure academic research should not be motivated by what seems to the researchers to be right or wrong in moral policy terms, but should be purely about establishing facts. Of course, these facts can (and in ASC often must) include assessing the feelings of the recipients of social care. There is a whole field of study devoted to trying to establish and quantify the value that ASC delivers. There is even an academic measure called SQRoL (sometimes pronounced "squirrel") for the purpose: it stands for Social Care Related Quality of Life.

For many people, such academic or policy engagement brings its own rewards – and, of course, if you get to play a leading role in this particular space, then you will also achieve **Fame** points and a degree of public recognition, writing public papers, giving speeches and mixing with influential public figures and politicians.

Finally, I come to:

Money

We all have to make a living. I was about to write that no-one enters ASC to get rich, but actually that's not entirely true. There have been many people, especially in the late 1980s and early 90s, who started businesses in the care home sector because they could see sizeable profits to be made. In some cases levels of care were not well maintained, and so government had to introduce tighter regulation and 'red tape' in order to ensure that vulnerable people were not being exploited. At the same time, local authorities, who fund approximately half the care home sector, started reducing the rates they were prepared to pay. Consequently costs increased and income declined, so that nowadays it's not easy (though still possible) to make money in this part of the sector.

In any sector at any time, if you are determined and make the right connections, then you can make a good living. A recent example of someone who has become a multi-millionaire in a closely related area is Emma Harrison, the founder and key shareholder of A4E, a company offering work training as well as improved access to health and social advisory services. In 2010 David Cameron appointed her 'Family Champion', and at the national social services conference in 2011, I heard her speak passionately about her company's role helping families with a history of unemployment to find their way back into work. Unfortunately, within four months, following a flurry of allegations of fraud and misuse of public funds, she was forced to resign both as government adviser and as chairman of A4E.

It had been an impressive money-spinner for her: in 2011 she earned £8.6 million in share dividends, in addition to her £365,000 annual salary, the majority of this having been funded by the taxpayer.

We will return to the important subject of leadership ethics in Chapter Thirteen.

Of course, not everyone is going to become a millionaire . . .

If you set yourself quite a high target in the last chapter as regards **Money**, don't be disheartened. There are plenty of ways of making a decent living in the sector and becoming really wealthy is over-rated in our society – it doesn't necessarily bring happiness. As a Senior Practitioner or Area Manager in a local authority you can earn well above the average income, and the same can be true in the commercial and not-for-profit sectors.

Equally important to earning a good income should be your work-life balance – particularly if you have or are starting a family of your own. Having your own children will cost a lot of time and money, but there are huge rewards both in the short and very long term, as long as you put in the time to really bond with and support them.

Of course, even if you have no intention of raising your own children, it's vital for your mental health that you keep time for friends, partners, hobbies, music, art, spiritual expression, etc.

I wish I could say that being in a caring profession such as ASC you will find it easier to achieve work-life balance than, say, in a purely commercial business. Sadly, this is not necessarily true. Just recently, I heard of a senior local government ASC manager who was very reluctant to tolerate part-time working amongst those she managed. Fortunately, this culture is now changing a little throughout society: there are, for example, now laws requiring all employers to consider part-time arrangements for parents, and granting the right to take time off (albeit unpaid) to look after children who are sick.

There are plenty of opportunities for part-time caring jobs in the sector, but they do tend to be at lower pay grades. The fact of the matter is that in any sector, if you want to move into a leading role of any kind, then you will have to be prepared to put in the hours, at least for significant stretches of your career. The trick is to find a field and vocation where that work brings satisfaction and a real degree of self-expression, not just the frustration of being at the beck and call of a lacklustre manager.

Be ready for the pressures

I've talked about the challenges as something positive, which will give you satisfaction to overcome, but do not be mistaken: ***there will be times when you struggle with the pressures and find that they start to get you down.***

Probably the biggest challenge in your early years will be dealing with the difficult situations that your clients and their carers face and realising that there is no magic wand to help them. You may find aspects of how some of your clients live hard to handle: for example, medical conditions with unsavoury complications such as incontinence, or their chaotic and seemingly just plain foolish way of life, should you be working with drug and alcohol addicts. Sometimes, even if you are well aware your clients have mental health problems, there may be times when you just feel like bashing their heads together. You will need all your resources of patience and empathy, but also the ability to keep a distance. It's essential that you have people with whom you can do some "off-loading", whether these be colleagues, professional supervisors, or friends (without, of course, infringing confidentiality).

Very often, you won't have access to the external resources that you believe will make that all-important difference to your clients. True, it's always the case that demand outstrips available resources, but this is particularly so in a time of financial austerity. Even if you are working with the minority of clients and carers who do have money to spend on care, it is in the nature of the work that many problems are simply intractable. By that I mean that even throwing all the money in the world at a client would not resolve their underlying problem. If someone has dementia, for example, then you should at least ensure they are looked after sensitively and that their carer has sufficient breaks for their own quality of life, but beyond these basic requirements just spending more and more is likely to bring rapidly diminishing returns.

There's certainly a very strong case to be made that a higher proportion of the Gross Domestic Product should be spent on adult social care – especially as the national demographic profile changes – but it is as well to accept from the outset that you will always want more time, more money, and more facilities to be available for your clients.

This brings us to bureaucracy. There is currently huge frustration amongst social workers, especially in children's services, at the amount of time they are obliged to spend on 'red tape' – form-filling, box-ticking, and entering data into computer systems. I will come back to the topic of bureaucracy and why a degree of it is inevitable, even desirable, in the chapter on being a DASS (Director of Adult Social Services), but this is not the book for an in-depth investigation of why social work involves a lot of form-filling and the exact degree to which that is appropriate.

Suffice to say that any professional role within the sector will inevitably involve a significant amount of bureaucratic tedium and you may well find this frustrating if you just want to focus on helping your clients.

Now, here's another Exercise.

We've focused on why you might be in Adult Social Care.

We've explored the different aspects of Heart, Brain, Money and Fame that might act as motivational drivers in your choice of career, you've thought about your own relationship to each of these, and we've briefly discussed paybacks and pressures.

Now, on the next page, write some notes about where you'd like your career in ASC to have brought you, first after 5 years, and then after 10 years. There are some guidelines to help you.

You may well have given this some thought already and talked it over with people. In that case, go right ahead and note down your ideas. There is, of course, no right or wrong answer – just what seems right and true to you at the moment. You also might not know yet what type of job or job description you would need to achieve your goal. Just write down some characteristics. What achievements would you hope to have under your belt by then?

If you haven't given this topic any thought at all before now, then this might be a good point to take a break from the book and allow your mind to mull it over. You could give it a day or two and come back to the exercise, or you could flick through other chapters in the book just to see if any ideas jump out at you, intrigue you, or catch your attention.

Exercise Three (a): My Five-Year Career Pathway

1) Where do I see myself in ASC in 5 years' time?

2) What will my life and career look like?

3) Am I likely to be working for the same employer?

4) Am I likely to be in the same town / city / country?

5) What will I have achieved?

6) What will be the paybacks I have gained?

7) Any particular pressures – private or job-related – that I might have overcome?

Next, think about your situation 10 years from now.

Why is Adult Social Care for you?

Exercise Three (b): My Ten-Year Career Pathway

1) I will be . . . years old
2) I expect / hope / will have a child/children who will be . . . years old

   or I do not expect to have children
3) I expect to have remained focused on my ASC career

   or to have taken a break for personal development or family responsibilities (children / parents)
4) I hope to have achieved a point in my career where I . . . *(describe some features)*

5) I expect to have received the following paybacks:-

6) I anticipate that, at some stage before reaching this point, I might have struggled with . . .

7) If this all comes to pass, I will feel . . .

When you've finished this book, you can refer back to these notes to see if anything has changed, and if you keep them carefully you'll be able to look back again in 5 and 10 years' time!

Chapter Three

Trust your Heart

OK, so you knew that social care was touchy-feely, but you really thought this book was going to give you more practical information instead of just asking you what you feel . . .

If you are feeling impatient, feel free to skip this section and go on to the next chapter.

The thing is, the older I get, the more I reckon it's important to fully acknowledge our heart desires and take them into account in our actions. And that is just as true for me as a man as it is for women.

Actually, the writing of this book provides a good example. I had planned to write something quite dry and factual. Then I went on the 'Book Midwife' course and it gave me the gift of realising that I do have something to say from my heart that does not require lots of research and that, hopefully, at least some of you will find useful, interesting and possibly even challenging.

We will be coming to more factual information, and to other people's stories, in the next chapter.

So what is the purpose of this section?

It's a sort of extension to the first chapter about how to use this book effectively, perhaps best expressed as '**How to use your life effectively**'.

The fact of the matter is that rational analysis of information is no longer enough.

a) The amount of information that is nowadays available to us means that there will always be far more available than we can absorb and process rationally.

b) Machines are getting better and better at processing lots of information and applying their implacable logic, but they will never be able to replace human intuition, empathy, spirit and emotional intelligence.

Increasingly, science gives us the capacity to prove rationally the very limits of rationality! There are some great examples in David Brooks' book *'The Social Animal – a story of how success happens'* (Short Books Ltd, 2nd revised edition 2012).

If you allow time and space for emotions, it will pay off.

You may not always know how it pays off. The pay-off might be as simple as avoiding an emotional or financial cost that you would otherwise incur later on.

In writing this book, I was very tempted to just dive in and start writing all the facts that I wanted to convey. Instead, I took the time to consider what message I wanted to get across, who I wanted to read the material and what their emotional as well as practical needs might be. I'd like to think that process has made this a more accessible, useful and enjoyable book. It has certainly made it easier and more fun to write.

Sometimes you just know what you have to do.

It might not be sensible. Some friends or family might tell you not to be so stupid – and they will do so out of genuine concern for you.

But if you are clear that there's something that you simply have to do, then those who love you deeply should be ready to let you go ahead – even if they expect to have to pick up the pieces. Hopefully, you'll be able not only to prove them wrong, but also

Making a Difference in Adult Social Care

grow through the experience.

Here I'd like to recount my own curious personal story, which has nothing directly to do with Adult Social Care:

Back in 2009 I decided to cycle through Zimbabwe dressed as a clown, bearing a personal message for President Mugabe.

Cartoon by Martijn Pantlin

Yes, you read that right, though it may mean little to you without me briefly describing the circumstances. Since 2000 the Zimbabwean Government of Robert Mugabe had been confiscating land from white farmers and re-allocating it to blacks. In order to retain power and justify the land re-distribution, the President had been whipping up anti-white and anti-British sentiment. In 2008 there was a presidential election, which Morgan Tsvangirai of the opposition MDC (Movement for Democratic Change) won in the first round. However, the ruling party, as well as rigging the vote, organised extensive atrocities and intimidation against the MDC. Consequently, Tsvangirai withdrew from the election rather than have his supporters continue to be beaten and killed. Political violence nonetheless continued all through 2008, whilst I was organising my bike ride. Zimbabwe, once the proudest and most developed of the black African countries, had become one of the poorest places in the world and I just wanted to help in some way. My plan was to raise money for a local charity benefitting AIDS orphans.

Apart from the violence, there were many reports of hunger and starvation. By Christmas 2008 there was a widespread outbreak of cholera. Despite this apparent descent into mayhem and chaos, most of my friends continued to actively support my good intentions. One friend, however, along with my sister, refused to condone what they thought was sheer reckless folly. Come the cholera epidemic, I nearly accepted their viewpoint, but I nonetheless persevered. There were at least some signs of improvement in the country, as a Government of National Unity was announced, at the behest of South Africa and other neighbouring countries.

In the event, the trip went off very smoothly and is one of the proudest achievements of my life. I've left up the website that we set up during the fundraising: *www.funzimride.co.uk*.

I really did have to trust my heart energy though – including the awareness that I was taking a message of reconciliation and healing rather than confrontation.

Be patient – and honest – with yourself

In writing this book I want you to think more about the future: about your future and how you can influence it. But don't put yourself under pressure to get there fast. Things have to take their time. Rome wasn't built in a day.

As I've noticed in my home town, when a Muslim community sets about constructing a new mosque it builds the basic structure so far as available funds permit, trusting that, 'inshallah' (God willing), the necessary money to fully realise the creative intention will be forthcoming in due course.

Although the end result may be different from what was originally anticipated, the journey will still be worthwhile and needs to be embarked on somehow. Remember Christopher Columbus, setting out to find a quick route to India and instead discovering a whole new continent!

On a rather more down-to-earth note, when I was extending my kitchen to modernize it and include a dining area, I engaged an architect. He duly came up with a plan, but his input gave me the confidence to develop my own vision. My builder got busy, and when he was part way through he suggested a significant improvement. We then incorporated this, discarding the architect's original design. One reason I love my new kitchen is that it is a manifestation of our creative process. Policy-making can be rather like this. It's important to set out a general direction of travel, then be open to improvements, even if the end result is not quite what was intended. We will come back to that theme later on, looking at various examples, in Chapter Twelve on policy making.

Find ways to explore the interplay of emotions with your mind and your body

Give yourself space for contemplation. Perhaps what works for you is a walk in the woods or by the river. You may like to try meditation. You might find your special space in your place of worship, if you have one.

It is now generally accepted that emotional factors have a direct physical impact and effect on the body. This can be difficult to acknowledge. For example, some childhood emotional trauma may have impacted on you physically, leaving you carrying it as a burden without being conscious of its origin.

To explore this interplay I recommend a physical activity that includes a high degree of conscious awareness. It may be yoga, Tae Kwondo, Tai Chi or some other form of martial art. If you're at all keen on dancing, the Five Rhythms practice offers a great way of unburdening through ecstatic movement. Do check out _www.acalltodance.com/5rhythms.htm_ or _www.schoolofmovementmedicine.com_.

Also be aware of what you consume. Alcohol, caffeine, and other drugs – even chocolate! – can all be great fun to use in social or other contexts. Just be conscious of how they affect your mood, both short- and longer-term. They can all mask or cut us off from our "heart energy".

In short, notice what energises you.

Let this be your guide, and try to follow it as much as you can.

Notice what does not energise you and try to avoid that.

Your energetic engagement – in earning your income, in your commitment to friends and family, in your own personal development – is dependent on you being conscious of, and actively cultivating, the things you need to sustain and nourish it.

Just try it – that's all I can say.

Chapter Four

Start with the big picture – how the ASC sector hangs together

The Adult Social Care sector is a large and complex one.

It will help your career to have a good overview. Whatever part of the sector you decide to devote yourself to, it's useful to understand the viewpoints of other stakeholders and actors.

When big corporations are recruiting for top executive trainees, they often insist that the new recruits spend time with the range of divisions and front-line roles within the company. This does not tend to happen in social work training but there is no reason why you cannot arrange it for yourself. I recommend trying to gain work experience in as many parts of the sector as possible. Even if it is only for one day of volunteering, you will find it worthwhile.

If you are already clear what line of career you wish to pursue, an overview of different roles will give you a clearer idea of your options.

As I've said, ASC is large and complex. We can quantify that, but first we need to define our terms. So far, we have talked about 'Adult Social Care' without establishing quite what that means.

Essentially, it is the full range of personal care and support for anyone, from age 18 through to death, who needs it because of some vulnerability or disability. It excludes purely medical care, although in practice the boundary is not always clear. (Indeed, something called 'Continuing Healthcare' is a prime example of a service that is defined as medical, thus enabling care and support to be funded free of charge through the NHS, although the type of care and support can be very similar to the means-tested service provided by a local authority's adult social services department.)

So we include in Adult Social Care:

* information, advice and guidance on support options.
* assessment of needs.
* support planning with the client and carer.
* delivery of equipment (e.g. wheelchair, stairlift) or home adaptations (e.g. downstairs shower, wheelchair ramp).
* delivery of personal care in the private home, including bathing, lifting in and out of bed, cooking, shopping, performing household tasks, all the way through to taking care of pets.
* respite care, to enable the client or the carer to 'get away from it all' for a hour or a week.
* residential care, from extra care provision with low level of support on call when needed through to full 24/7 secure nursing care.
* Increasingly, we should also include financial planning for frailty in old age to be part of social care.

Sometimes we just refer to providing 'care & support', but the word 'social' is an important one: it reminds us that we are all social animals and a key part of our needs is to be able to interact with friends, family and others around us. This has to be borne in mind during support planning. Also, the social web around a person can often provide an important source of informal care and support; occasionally, it may itself be a source of problems needing to be addressed.

Now we have defined our terms, let's quantify the size of the ASC sector.

Financial

Local authorities in England spent £17 billion on Adult Social Care in 2010-11, although this has reduced to £14 billion for 2013-14 (inclusive of client contributions to their care costs).

An additional £11.7 billion was spent by the national government in England on Disability Living Allowance and Attendance Allowance. Together that equates to more than 2% of the total Gross Domestic Product for England.

The amount of money the state spends on older people (i.e. those over 65) is particularly impressive:

- ✔ NHS → £49 billion
- ✔ Social care → £8.4 billion
- ✔ Social security benefits (including pensions and disability benefits) → £82.6 billion.

(figures for 2009/10 from *'Fairer Care Funding: The Report of the Commission on Funding Care and Support'*, a.k.a *The Dilnot Report*, July 2011.)

£4 billion is spent in England by local authorities on adults of working age with learning difficulties (*NHS Information Centre report for 2009-10*). The expenditure on social care for people with physical disabilities, mental health problems or drug and alcohol addictions is approximately £2 billion per annum.

However, local authority spending is only a proportion of all the money spent on Adult Social Care, as only approximately 40% of those needing ASC qualify on grounds of income and level of need. Estimates of how much 'self-funders' spend on their own care are difficult to come by but a conservative estimate would place it at £8 billion per annum in England.

It should be borne in mind that informal carers contribute £119 billion worth of care (*www.carers.org.uk*) – in other words, if they were not offering their services for free, that is how much it would theoretically cost local authorities. This assessment might seem invidious because it starts to put a monetary value on what we should expect to be the natural human function of looking after our own family members. It is, nonetheless, an interesting statistic and I can understand why the Carers Society promotes it as a way of highlighting the importance of carers in society. The danger is that it starts to imply that all carers should be entitled to something like that level of compensation from the state. This leads us into a wider moral, social and political discussion, which I will set aside for another time.

What is less contentious is that an estimated 300,000 carers have dropped out of employment in order to care for an elderly or disabled loved one, at a cost of £5.3 billion to the economy and £1 billion in lost taxation revenue, according to a 2012 Age UK report.

These vast figures are hard to conceptualise, so the following graphic might help. It comes from the World Alzheimer Report 2010, and shows the worldwide cost of dementia in relation to the annual turnover of some famously monied corporations.

THE COST OF DEMENTIA WORLDWIDE

Artwork courtesy of Rita Branco

These figures demonstrate just how economically significant ASC spending is, on a local, national, and even international level. Many of the people delivering low paid domiciliary care or working in residential homes are immigrants sending remittances back to their families abroad. (The European Union even sponsors a programme specifically to assist immigrants working in EU social care, called CASA.)

I came across an interesting statistic a few years ago: two out of every five women work in the caring professions. This proportion includes all forms of care, including medical care and teaching, but is nonetheless still a high number. Amongst women of black and minority ethnic origin the proportion apparently increases to three out of every five.

This brings us onto the next section.

Numbers involved in Adult Social Care in England

In England there are more than one and a half million people working in the ASC sector.

In September 2011 there were 160,300 people employed in adult social services departments, 9% of the sector's total.

Of these, only 10% (16,300) were social worker jobs. Interestingly, the number of social worker jobs is estimated to have remained stable over the preceding year while the number of other jobs in council social care has dropped by around 7%.

The majority (82 %) of adult social services jobs in 2011 were carried out by female workers, 18% by males.

The average age of these adult social services employees was 47.

(Source: *'Personal Social Services: Staff of social services departments'*, The NHS Information Centre, 2012)

An estimated 21,900 organisations are involved in providing or organising adult social care and 48,300 establishments employ care staff. (*Skills for Care News Release,* 1 September 2011).

Every year councils receive more than 2 million new contacts requesting social care support. Half of these result in further assessment or ongoing services.

The number of assessments in 2010-11 was 661,000. Of these, 68% went on to receive services as a result of their assessment.

The difference is down to the fact that, whilst anyone is entitled to request an initial assessment from the LA, you will only receive LA help if your needs exceed a specified threshold *and* your income and capital are below a certain level. It is a fair assumption that everyone who receives an LA assessment has some kind of social care need.

These statistics are likely to change significantly from April 2016 when the care funding reforms take effect (along the lines recommended by the Dilnot Report). Many more contacts will progress to an assessment, because people will be entitled to a 'cap' on their total care costs, i.e. there will be a limit on the total amount that they have to pay for their care. Above that limit, the state (through the local authority) will absorb the cost. However, your care costs will only count towards that limit once you have been assessed by your local authority as having needs above the threshold of entitlement.

In 2010-11 the total number of people receiving services was 1.6 million, which can be broken down as follows:

* Community based services: 1.3 million
* Residential care: 213,000
* Nursing care: 88,000

These figures include 377,000 people receiving 'self directed support', of whom 125,000 received a direct payment (up 17% from 2009-10).

The number of carers receiving services was 380,000. Of these, 50% received a carer specific service and 50% received information only.

(Source: *'Community Care Statistics: Social Services Activity, England –*

2010-11', NHS Information Centre, 2012)

In summary, approximately 1 in 20 of all adults are in receipt of a social care service from their local council.

In addition, there are many people who do not want to bother the council or who know they have sufficient financial means to make them ineligible for support. This group accounts for an additional 170,000 or so in care homes or nursing homes and 270,000 paying for their own care at home.

The total size of the self-funded care market is significant:

* The home care market has grown from an estimated £510 million in 2002-2003 to £652 million in 2010.
* The care home market for older people in England is estimated to be £4.9 billion.

Both estimates exclude people who 'top-up' a council-funded care home place, which could account for an additional £1.15 billion.

(*Report by the Institute of Public Care*, Oxford Brookes University, 2010)

Thus, total adult social care expenditure in England is well in excess of £21 billion per annum.

In the longer term occupational pensions and the value of housing equity held by many older people are likely to take large numbers out of state funding, given current thresholds. For example, by 2030 a third of Herefordshire's population will be aged 65 or over, with more than 80% being home owners. These will be the main beneficiaries of the care funding reforms due to the cap on total private care expenditure and the fact that the capital limit of the means test is also being raised.

(*People Who Pay for Care*, Putting People First Consortium, 2011)

The Carers Society estimates that there are 6 million people across the UK providing informal care, of whom 1.25 million provide more than 50 hours per week.

The Community Care online magazine for March 2013 provided the following update:

> **Adult social worker jobs and pay increase while councils cut back on other care staff**
>
> * Councils employed 2% more adult social workers in 2012 than 2011 despite a 5% cut in the adult social services workforce overall according to the annual workforce data published by the Health & Social Care Information Centre.
> * Median annual salaries for social workers also increased by 2%, from £31,200 to £31,800.
> * The overall drop in staff numbers was attributed to budget cuts, staff restructuring and outsourcing of services.
>
> Other findings from the research indicated that:
>
> * 79% of social workers (and 82% of the whole adult social services workforce) were female.
> * The average age of social workers in 2012 was 45, compared with 47 for the workforce as a whole.
> * 19% of social workers were from black and minority ethnic groups, up from 18% in 2011, and compared with a whole workforce figure of 12%.
> * 51% of all adult social services jobs were part-time, compared to 29% of professional positions in general.
> * Adult social services staff employed by councils made up just 8% of the wider adult social care workforce in England. 49% were employed by the private sector, 16% by the voluntary sector and 23% directly by service users.

Complexity

Even professionals sometimes struggle to understand the complexities of care and support. There are many 'vertical' specialisms within social care, e.g. Occupational Therapists (OTs), Approved Mental Health Professionals (for Mental

Health Act purposes), Independent Mental Capacity Advocates, Learning Difficulty Support Workers, Addiction Specialists, Financial Assessors, Mobility Aids Advisers, not to mention all the various medical roles.

In Chapter Six we'll be hearing about Meg Barbour's husband, who suffered from dementia. In the course of this relatively straightforward case, over three years, all of the following were involved:

- The GP
- The Memory Clinic
- A lawyer who advised on the enduring power of attorney
- A Community Psychiatric Nurse
- A Flexible Carer from Age Concern (now Age UK)
- A Carers Support Worker from the Alzheimer's Society
- Day care staff
- Staff at another day centre offering respite care

- Home care staff specializing in dementia and lifting
- A Social Worker who made a needs and financial assessment
- An equipment installer
- The residential care home manager and her staff, including a nurse
- A specialist dementia doctor.

Incidentally, this human complexity is one of the reasons why information systems in adult social care are difficult to implement comprehensively. (That was my background before I set up my own consultancy company.)

Overview of ASC organisational stakeholders

We can also represent the sector from the viewpoint of the various interested organisations. Let's start with:

Local Authorities (LAs)

LAs have responsibility for:

- ✓ providing advice and guidance on ASC to all their citizens.
- ✓ carrying out an assessment of care needs on any citizen who requests it.
- ✓ supplying care and support to anyone in their area who has been assessed and whose needs are above the locally determined eligibility threshold.
- ✓ recovering the costs of care from those clients who can afford to contribute.
- ✓ managing the financial affairs of those clients who do not themselves have sufficient mental capacity (and no informal carers available to act in that role).
- ✓ devising long-term Public Health planning and campaigns (one of the provisions of the 2012 Health & Social Care Act).
- ✓ reporting to central government on their performance, via the NHS Information Centre.

✓ encouraging a choice of private and third sector care provision for all citizens, whether funded by the LA or purchased by 'self-funders'.

The Social Care Bill, published as draft in July 2012, adds to and modifies the responsibilities of LAs.

Within the LA itself there are a range of roles. Overall responsibility for local policy and decisions lies with:

Councillors – also known as 'Elected Members'

(Or 'Members' for short, and yes, this can lead to a few jokes and puns . . .)

Following the local authority reorganisation a few years ago, a single councillor, rather than a committee as hitherto, holds responsibility as cabinet member for Adult Social Services. There is also a scrutiny committee, which includes councillors from the opposition parties who can check and question the cabinet member's decisions.

In practice, the cabinet member is closely advised by the

Director of Adult Social Services (DASS)

This is a statutory post with legal responsibility for all the LA's adult social care staff and spending. It's a significant position: ASC costs may account for between 35% to 60% of the whole council budget. Sometimes their actual title will vary and, especially in unitary authorities, may be combined with other sectors such as Housing, Libraries or Children's Services.

Briefly, in England there are 3 types of local authorities:

- unitary authorities

and two-tier authorities consisting of:

- County Councils, and within them: * District Councils

In Wales and Scotland, all councils have been unitary authorities since the local government reorganisations in the 1990s.

In two-tier authority areas, the County Council retains responsibility for the major spending portfolios: Social Care (Adults and Children), Education and Highways. Counties come in various sizes, ranging in population from under 300,000 to over 1.3 million people. Within each County Council there are between three and seven District Councils, each responsible for Refuse Collection, Housing, Planning, Council Tax collection, Housing Benefit, Trading Standards, etc.

Each type of council has its own elected members. In the last two decades there has been a slow trend (now stopped) towards more unitary authorities.

A unitary authority combines all the responsibilities of local government into one body. Although this may be more efficient, the centralisation of decision-making does take its toll on local autonomy. There are three types of unitary authority:

- London Boroughs
- Metropolitan Boroughs created in the 70s, generally urban
- The newer unitary authorities created from the Local Government Reorganisations beginning in the 1990s and only just completed in 2010.

To return to the ASC roles within an LA, under the DASS there will be a number of Assistant Directors or deputies. Actual job titles and responsibilities vary but they can be split into four categories:

→ **commissioning**: the responsibility for awarding and monitoring contracts with external care providers. This accounts for the major part of the budget, although with with the introduction of personal budgets and direct payments the proportion is slightly declining.

→ **assessment and support planning**: this is the area that most qualified social workers operate in, carrying out assessment of needs, helping clients and carers put together a support plan, and ensuring that it can be delivered in accordance with its policies within the LA budget. Incidentally, a succession of legal challenges has established the principle that the LA does have a legal obligation to provide care, as long as the person's overall needs are above the eligibility threshold.

→ **internal service delivery**: LAs still employ some of their own internal staff to deliver care at home, although these days this is usually only as part of a 're-ablement phase'. Most LAs run their own day centres (although the numbers are declining) and many still have their own residential care homes, though mostly these were sold off to the private sector in the late 1990s and early 2000s.

→ **internal support services**: Human Resources, IT, Finance, Policy.

Oh, and then we now have Directors of Public Health (DPHs), another statutory role with specific duties in law (transferred from the NHS to LAs with effect from April 2013). The DPH will either be line managed by the DASS or may report directly to the LA's Chief Executive.

Of course, beneath the Assistant Directors (or ADs) we have a range of intermediate managers. These can be organised by geography, especially in the larger authorities, where you might have an Area Manager for each of North, South and Central districts. Or they might be organised by client group specialism: Older People (i.e. over 65s), Learning Difficulty, Mental Health, Physical Disability, Drug and Alcohol.

Then there are all the hundreds of frontline staff who interact directly with the citizens in need of care and support. These consist of social workers, administrative support, finance officers, care workers, occupational therapists and a whole range of other job titles.

Starting from the top of the organisational sector, we have:

The Department of Health

This is part of what is collectively known as 'Whitehall', because government headquarters used to be in the street called Whitehall in Westminster, central London. Nowadays offices are spread around central London and the regions. The Department of Health is now largely located in Leeds, though Ministers and their policy advisers remain in Westminster, conveniently close to Parliament.

The Department of Health for England is responsible for setting policy and providing much of the money that LAs spend on ASC. (The rest of the money spent on ASC by LAs comes from Council Tax and local business rates.)

Policy includes writing and amending laws, which then have to be agreed with Parliament, but that is only the tip of a large iceberg. The Department (in the name of the Secretary of State for Health) has the power to issue policy directives to LAs about how they should run ASC. Its legal powers are limited because LAs are independent and under the control of their own elected members. Usually the Department issues only 'guidance' which LAs have no legal obligation to implement, although most will. Part of the funding may be dependent on the LA demonstrating they have implemented this guidance. Sometimes funding is available to only a few LAs, who are required to bid for the money in competition with other LAs by showing that they have the best ideas for delivering a new piece of policy. This is an approach often used if the government wants to test the effectiveness of new ways of working, allowing for fine-tuning before encouraging the roll-out to other areas. One example of this was the Common Assessment Framework Demonstrator Site Programme.

The 2010-11 budget for DH is £102 billion ongoing expenditure and £4.4 billion capital expenditure. Most of this goes directly to the NHS. There are a couple of dozen staff who work on social care policy, including commissioning research, running trial

Making a Difference in Adult Social Care

projects and advising LAs and others across the sector.

No doubt inspired by the government's constant emphasis on the setting and meeting of targets, the diagram below is how the Department of Health would like us to visualise its structure and purpose. Concentric rings, framed by government direction and legislation, focus inward through successive layers of monitoring, supervision and administration, all the way to the cradle-to-grave care enjoyed by the fortunate British public.

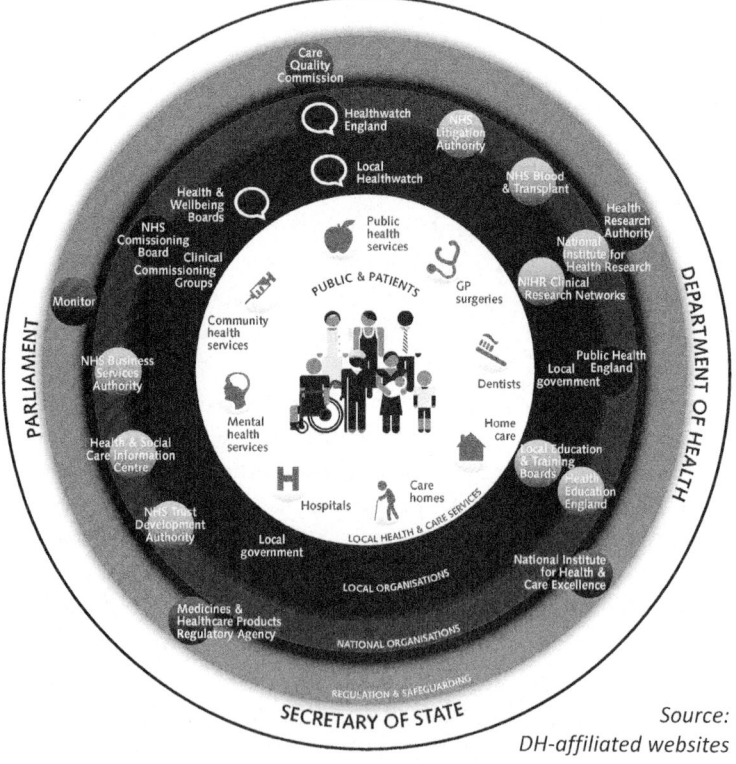

Source: DH-affiliated websites

At the top of DH sit the

Ministers

There are currently five Ministers as below (with the names at time of writing):

How the ASC sector hangs together

Title & Rank	Portfolio	Postholder in 2013
Secretary of State	Overall responsibility	The Rt Hon Jeremy Hunt MP (Con)
Minister of State	Care services, mental health, disabilities	Norman Lamb MP (Lib Dem)
Parliamentary Under Secretary of State	Health Services	Daniel Poulter MP (Con)
Parliamentary Under Secretary of State	Public health, devolved matters	Anna Soubry MP (Con)
Parliamentary Under Secretary of State	Quality, primary care, NHS Constitution, medicines	The Earl Howe (Con)

The Secretary of State has overall responsibility for this sprawling department. He is a member of the Cabinet, the topmost level of the UK government executive, as chaired by the Prime Minister. Although the Secretary of State will consult with other Cabinet members on major issues of public interest across health and social care he (or she) enjoys direct personal say-so over much of health and social care policy. For example, and controversially, the Secretary of State has a legal duty to deliver the National Health Service. This was to have been amended by the 2012 Health & Social Care Act but, following a public outcry, has remained in place.

From 2010 to September 2012 the Secretary of State was Andrew Lansley. During the Labour Governments of Tony Blair and Gordon Brown he spent six years as 'Shadow' Health Secretary, meaning that his job was to challenge the government on its health policy and develop alternative proposals for the Conservatives to implement should they win the next election. Usually, the top politicians move around the different 'portfolios' or top jobs in order to develop a range of experience (which would stand them in good stead should they aspire to become Prime Minister). In contrast, Andrew Lansley hung on to his shadow portfolio for an exceptionally long time, not only demonstrating a high degree of personal commitment but also developing an in-depth knowledge of the sector. When the Conservatives formed the Coalition Government with the Liberal Democrats in May 2010, he was the 'man with a plan': the result was the highly controversial Health and Social Care Act, passed into law in 2012.

There are many good reasons why the Bill generated extremely heated opposition, not least the fact that it was contrary to the Conservative election manifesto, which promised an end to top-down reorganisation of the NHS. I have seen and heard Andrew Lansley at consecutive annual conferences on social care, observing him progress from being an impassioned but powerless opposition spokesman, through the exuberance of being a Cabinet bigwig, all the way to being the most vilified of government ministers. There is no doubt in my mind that he did have a genuine passion for improving the efficiency and local responsiveness of the NHS. Perhaps naively, he was taken aback by the vehemence of the opposition and was clearly personally worn down by it. The Act features significant measures to improve local integration between the health service and LA social care via the Health and Wellbeing Boards. Transferring responsibility for Public Health to LAs allows for greater democratic accountability and should enable better long-term planning in conjunction with housing, leisure provision and social care. However, for most health professionals, these positives have been far outweighed by the incessant upheaval, threat of job losses and, most worryingly, the increasing opportunities for private companies to make profits out of the health service.

I've included this aside about Andrew Lansley and the 2012 H&SC Act because he was the supreme head of Adult Social Care in the country. Whatever you might think of his policies, you may find it interesting to have a very brief picture of the man and the personal difficulties of that position. You needn't feel too sorry for him though. My prediction is that he will retire from Cabinet level politics before the next election and, in due course, take up a number of well-paid directorships with private health companies.

Below the Secretary of State we have:

The Minister of State for Social Care

He or she is also an elected Member of Parliament (or else, perhaps, a member of the House of Lords). The Minister of State has overall responsibility for all policy issues regarding social care in England, together with any changes to the law, guidance or funding from national government that might be needed. On the bigger issues they will consult closely with the Secretary of State, who retains legal responsibility, but for the specifics of social care policy it is he or she who is responsible.

The current (2013) and previous ministers are both Lib Dem MPs, Norman Lamb and Paul Burstow. Like most of the better and longer-lasting social care ministers, they both have a background as Local Authority councillors. Norman Lamb was Leader of Norwich Council and Paul Burstow had responsibility for social services in the London Borough of Sutton. This means they have a thorough understanding of the issues. Both had been health spokesmen for the Lib Dems in opposition. An important part of any minister's job is travelling around the country meeting the professionals and public who are most affected by their policy: specifically, in this case, social workers, providers of social care services, disabled people, frail elderly people, carers, etc. It is important that all of these have the sense that their real concerns have been appreciated.

Ministers with a background of knowledge and experience in their field also benefit from being better able to stand up to their civil service advisers.

Every Secretary of State has a **Permanent Secretary**

And the Minister of State has a

Director General of Social Care

Don't be fooled by the name – the Permanent Secretary doesn't make the tea and keep the Minister's appointment book. He or she is in fact the most senior career civil servant in the Department of Health, with responsibility for the day-to day operational management of the whole department.

In every government Department of State (Health, the Home Office, Work and Pensions, International Development, etc) there is a Permanent Secretary. Each of these has a number of Director Generals (DGs) to act as their deputies, with responsibilities for specific areas.

Until 2006 Adult Social Care was not considered important enough to have its own DG, so it was considered a result for the sector when, in September 2006, David Behan was appointed as the first one. His background had been in local government (Director of Social Services at Richmond) rather than Whitehall, and he went on to develop close working relationships with DASS's and a network of Regional Directors. He transformed the sector by driving through Individual Budgets (now named Personal Budgets) and Personalisation. After six years at the helm of English ASC, he moved on to be Chief Executive of the Care Quality Commission, which regulates both health and care services.

Regulators and Quangos

In addition to his own pool of civil servants, the DG will advise the Minister on appointments to a range of regulatory bodies and 'quangos'. A quango is a 'Quasi Non-Governmental Organisation', which means that although it is set up and funded by the government it has a duty to be independent. There are many quangos set up to regulate different business sectors, for example, Ofgem, the Office of Gas & Electricity Markets, which is supposed, amongst other things, to make sure that electricity and gas companies charge fair prices. Even after the Coalition Government's so-called 'bonfire of the quangos', shortly after they came to power, there still remain several in the health and social care sector.

The main regulator in Adult Social Care is the

Care Quality Commission

This body is responsible for ensuring that every organisation delivering care in the ASC and Health sectors does so in accordance with prescribed minimum standards. It deploys a small army of inspectors to go round checking that care homes, home care agencies, hospital, dentists, etc, are performing acceptably. These have the power to remove the licence to operate from both private companies and local government departments.

It is a somewhat thankless task as private companies see the inspectors as intrusive and bothersome, inevitably adding to their bureaucratic burden. At the same time, CQC's resources are constrained and have not grown to match the wider remit they have been given since 2009. Inevitably, there will be instances of very poor performance that escape CQC's attention. They have recently, quite rightly, emphasized that they alone cannot be responsible for upholding minimum standards; it has to be the responsibility of everyone working in and using the sector to ensure qood quality and report any lapses to CQC, who then can take appropriate action. Unfortunately, there have been one or two instances over recent years where they were not seen to take action rapidly enough: e.g. Castlebeck hospital. The CQC was only set up in its current form in 2009, with the quirky Cynthia Bower as their chief executive. She steered the organisation through difficult times, including a significant expansion of duties on a limited budget, but resigned as CQC chair in February 2012 after a parliamentary grilling and losing the support of one or two members of her management board.

Another important quango in the sector is:

NICE

The National Institute for Clinical Excellence, for which this neat acronym acts as signifier, has now had its function extended to represent the National Institute for Health and Care Excellence. It is, nonetheless, considered not NICE but nasty by many members of the public suffering from certain diseases, who find their access to all-important drugs denied. Its primary duty is to investigate whether new medical treatments are both effective and good value for money. It has a necessarily complex way of assessing this based around the principle of 'qualy', an acronym standing for 'quality of life years'. This is a measure not just of whether a particular medicine or procedure keeps patients alive for longer, but of the degree and extent over time to which it improves their quality of life.

Because the NHS is entirely government-funded by taxation and is free to all citizens at the point of delivery, there has to be some mechanism to decide whether certain drugs and treatments should be available. Inevitably, demand will always outstrip what can be afforded. If your child or partner is ill, you will want done whatever it takes to make them well or extend their life, no matter how slight the amelioration or brief the remission might be. If the government is footing the bill, why not expect the very best possible treatment? If we lived in a pure, but harsh, free market economy then you would have to pay for every treatment. Unless you were extremely wealthy, there would be a strict limit on what you could afford. The apparent unfairness of this is mitigated, in countries like the USA where there is much more of a free market in healthcare, by health insurance companies, which spread the risk of costs incurred from sickness or accident and clarify the expense and types of treatments available.

In the UK, guidance and decisions on such matters are provided by NICE, which makes its calculations by setting the cost of the treatment against its value in terms of 'qualys' that it on average adds to a patient. Of course, they don't always get it right and sometimes their research does not keep up with scientific and practical developments, but, on balance, they do provide an essential service. (There is also an argument that they are too focused on the purely scientific and therefore do not recognise the value of complementary and alternative health treatments such as homeopathy, even though many thousands of people claim these to be beneficial.)

Finally, although NICE carries out the research and provides guidance, the actual decision on whether to fund treatments is taken at a more local level – prior to April 2013 by the Primary Care Trusts. These have now been abolished under the 2012 Health & Social Care Act and replaced by Clinical Commissioning Groups (CCGs) led by GPs. This means that GPs will become responsible for the inevitable rationing decisions in the NHS – something that many GPs fear will damage their reputation and put them in conflict with some patients whose treatments will not be funded.

This digression into the area of the NHS is because in April 2013 NICE took on the responsibility to provide evidence-based social care guidance as well as evaluating medical interventions. (I also thought it important for you to understand how medicines are currently rationed.) The methodology is likely to build on work with 'squirrels'.

No, I don't mean the furry animals that scamper around the trees in our parks and gardens, I'm referring to 'SCRQol' – the 'Social Care Related Quality of Life', a measure of how much social care interventions have improved the recipients' quality of life, rather like qualy. The concept has been developed by academics at Kent and other universities as part of the Personal Social Services Research Unit (PSSRU).

SCIE – The Social Care Institute for Excellence

The Social Care Institute for Excellence is legally an independent charity but historically was for the most part directly funded by the Department of Health. Since the passage of the H&SC Act in 2012 it will be funded through NICE and will have to bid for contracts. Its role is to provide advice and guidance on the best ways to deliver care to the ASC sector. In the past this has been available to all health and social care professionals, including the private sector, but it is now expanding its role to provide advice and guidance to the general public through the Find Me Good Care website. See *www.scie.org.uk* and *www.findmegoodcare.co.uk*.

Other quangos include:

The Health and Care Professions Council maintains a register of social workers and other care professionals and has the power to strike off anyone found acting unprofessionally, barring them from continuing to work in that profession. See *www.hpc-uk.org.*

The Health and Social Care Information Centre compiles statistics on care delivery from councils, hospitals and other bodies, and is the definitive source of information about health and social care provision. See *www.hscic.gov.uk*.

The College of Social Work (*www.tcsw.org.uk*) and the **British Association of Social Workers** (*www.basw.co.uk*) are competing professional organisations claiming to represent the voice of social work and offering benefits to members.

The National Health Service

Of course, describing the complexity and workings of the NHS could take up a whole book in itself, so I will be very brief and focus on its interaction with ASC.

For the general public, the main or primary touchpoint with the NHS is through their General Practice doctor (GP). GPs almost always operate in a shared practice, which comprises a number of GPs along with administrative and support staff including nurses. Each practice is a legally independent commercial organisation, normally in the form of a partnership between the principal GPs (who will employ other GPs on a salary). They are paid by the NHS through a complex range of tariffs based on the number of patients they have and the appointments and treatments they provide.

GPs are collectively referred to as **Primary Care**. Some practices, with the encouragement of their Local Authority, are starting to co-operate closely with social workers. Increasingly it is the GP who suggests to a patient that they should seek social care support from the council.

'**Secondary Care**' in the jargon refers to hospitals. (It is secondary because it is the second place you come to following a referral from your doctor – unless it is an Accident & Emergency case!) Hospitals vary widely in terms of size and specialism but we all know broadly what they are like. There used to be many more small community hospitals but in the 1980s most of these were closed, on the grounds that either bigger hospitals or providing appropriate treatment in patients' own homes would be more efficient. Hospitals are constitutionally separate Trusts within the NHS, with their own Chief Executives and Boards.

'**Community Health**' refers to the network of nurses, OTs, midwives, health visitors, etc who look after people in their own homes. Many recipients of social care in their homes also rely on medical care from community health. Organisationally, community health used to be delivered mainly by Primary Care Trusts (PCTs) but is now being delivered by separate Trusts or merged with existing Health Trusts.

'**Mental Health**' is the other main area of the NHS. There are separate mental hospital trusts for people suffering the acute stages of a wide range of mental health problems, from depression, through personality disorder, to bi-polar disorder and schizophrenia. The MH trusts also run Community Mental Health Teams, which for many years now have combined social workers (paid by the LA) with psychiatrists and Community Psychiatric Nurses (CPNs). In addition to providing some care, support and diagnosis, these teams can detain people for treatment under the Mental Health Act.

Finally, we come to the non-governmental sector of ASC, which can be divided into the private commercial sector and the not-for-profit charity or social enterprise sector, although in practice the recipient of a service may not always be able to detect any difference as to whether it is delivered by one or the other.

The private sector

Private businesses provide a whole range of care and support services including:

- residential care homes and nursing homes
- home care, a.k.a. 'domiciliary care', a.k.a. 'support at home'
- day centres
- mobility aids
- telecare equipment, e.g. alarm systems.

The advent of Personal Budgets has given individuals more control over how their council funding of their care is spent. It has encouraged the growth of new micro-businesses in particular niche areas, such as arranging holidays for people with disabilities. Break Barriers CIC in Nottingham is just one such example (*www.breakbarrierscic.com*).

Some of the established businesses are very large commercial organisations, e.g.:

- **BUPA**, which employs over 62,000 people worldwide and operates 300 care homes in the UK.
- **Anchor Trust**, with a not-for-profit turnover of £264 million in 2012 and more than 30,000 people in retirement homes owned or managed by them.

- **Barchester**, which accepts only private clients, not LA-funded ones, in its 220 locations.
- **SAGA**, originally known for organising holidays for older people, now also offers home care services.
- **Southern Cross**, which achieved notoriety following its September 2011 announcement that it was pulling out of the care home market. The Association of Directors of Adult Social Services (ADASS) had to step in and help manage the transfer of homes or residents to other organisations.

There are also a very large number of small family businesses running one, two or three care homes or a home care service employing between twenty and fifty care workers in a particular locality. It's a competitive business, with LAs increasingly pushing down the rates they are prepared to pay and companies unwilling to pay many of their staff much above the minimum wage. In many areas of the country it is also very reliant on immigrant labour.

Social Enterprises and Charities

The service delivered by a social enterprise may be identical to that of a private business. The difference is that they are set up specifically to provide for a sector of the population rather than to make a capital gain for their owners. Legally, they are Community Interest Companies, a fairly new form of limited company introduced by the last Labour Government. They are normally 'asset locked', which means that the assets or capital of the company can only be used for the benefit of the community which it has been set up to serve. The company is not permitted to pay dividends to private shareholders nor be sold off to profit them.

Charities such as Age UK, MIND, Scope, Alzheimer's Society, Marie Curie Cancer Care, Carers Association, etc., tend to have multiple functions. They all deliver services for their client groups throughout the country and usually receive funding from LAs or the NHS to do so. They also raise their own funds to provide services and to lobby and campaign for improved arrangements for their client groups. Some of them also invest in their own research, e.g. the Alzheimer's Society and various cancer trusts.

There is more on Social Enterprises and Charities in Chapter Ten, but first I want to talk about the people in charge of making local authority social care decisions.

Chapter Five

Local political leadership – being a Councillor

This may seem a strange place to start going through the options for taking a leading role in ASC. You might think that being a counsellor, advising people about their personal problems, is more relevant to social care than being a councillor, an elected member on a local authority. It is true that a councillor is not necessarily engaged with ASC at all. So why would I start here? More importantly, why would *you* start here?

Yes, I *am* suggesting you may want to start a career in ASC by being a councillor for a while, and here's why:

1) We need more younger councillors!
2) Standing for election as a councillor will make you focus on what your real values are.
3) As a councillor (and in campaigning) you will meet a wide range of people and will need to appreciate and relate to their concerns.
4) You will have a personal case load that will include some people with social care issues (at least if you are a councillor in an authority with social services responsibility –

see below).

5) It will give you a broader understanding and more credibility later in your career.

Also, councillors are collectively responsible for £17 billion of ASC spending in England.

Before we take these points one by one, I should point out that there are other ways to combine an interest in local politics and care issues: for example, campaigning on local issues, becoming active with your local Healthwatch group (see previous chapter), taking part in local consultations, volunteering.

We need more younger councillors

All political parties find it hard to recruit people who are prepared to stand as councillors. Being a councillor can be very time-consuming, with minimal financial reward. In 2013 Oxfordshire County Council offered an allowance of £8,295 per annum, with cabinet members receiving an additional £12,442 for what can be pretty much a full time job. It's not surprising that many councillors are retired people. The average age of councillors has increased from 55 in 1997 to 60 in 2010. (*LGA website*)

It was not always like this. In the 1980s, when I was in my twenties, there were quite a few of my generation who became councillors. I put it down largely to the fact that there was much more interest in politics – and especially party politics – than there is today.

This offers you an opportunity: it is now not difficult to become a councillor if you set your mind to it. This chapter offers some practical steps as to how to achieve this goal.

Another reason why fewer people wish to enter local politics is that local councils have significantly fewer powers than they used to have. Whereas central government tends to be quite prescriptive, a large part of local government is simply concerned with the effective administration of national policies. Nevertheless, local councils do control significant spending budgets, greater than many sizeable businesses. Budgets range from the £29 million disbursed by the small unitary authority of Rutland County Council to the whopping £1.8 billion administered by Kent County Council.

Local government is the bedrock of democracy; it is vital that the younger generations remain involved and committed to it, contributing their freshness of ideas and approach. Democracy is an absolutely essential counter-balance to the consumer marketplace, in determining how we operate as a society and what our shared values might be.

Politics is an under-valued art. It is about representing a section of society and then brokering solutions to social problems with the representatives of various other sections of society.

Of course, younger people *do* have some say in this process, via the media (including social media) and through voting once every so often. One can also argue that new forms of local democracy are long overdue. In the meantime, whilst bureaucratic sectional party politics may be on the wane, local government is here to stay and needs locally elected representatives from all ages and sections of society.

Clarify your values

Social care is about values. Faced with challenging situations, you need to be very clear on where you stand. It will help you to hone your own value systems by having to justify your opinions on doorstep after doorstep, engaging in debate within your political organisation, providing clear statements in your published material and, having been elected, in your deliberations in the council chamber and committees.

The greatest value that you will need to practice, the one that, regardless of your political persuasion, will stand you in best stead in an ASC career, is showing respect for your constituents.

Meeting a wide range of people

We all tend to inhabit quite a narrow social circle. When thrown into a large social pool, we instinctively seek out people with whom we feel comfortable, people like ourselves, who went to the same sort of school, or who come from the same part of the world. In campaigning to be elected you have to get out there and talk to all sorts of people on the doorstep. As a councillor, you are expected to be available to help any of your constituents with their particular concerns and troubles.

This will give you a wide-ranging understanding of people's issues and concerns – some of which might surprise you!

A caseload including social care issues

Some of your constituents' concerns will relate to adult social care, depending on what sort of council you are serving on. In the previous chapter, in the section on DASS's, I explained about unitary authorities and two-tier councils. If you live in a two-tier county area and you want to get involved in adult social care issues as a councillor, you should get yourself elected onto the county council, not the district or city council. The disadvantage here is that county council elections are held only once every four years, while unitary council elections come around with greater frequency.

The thought of having a high caseload, with a heavy burden of other people's problems weighing down on your shoulders, might be off-putting, but – apart from preparing you for life as a social worker, if that is your path – it **doesn't** actually have to be quite so onerous. Don't tell everyone, but many councillors manage to keep their personal caseloads down to only two or three per month, and there are council officers paid to help you process your casework. There is one advantage in being a county councillor rather than a district or unitary councillor: people won't be able to bother you with complaints about bin collections, rubbish in the streets or planning applications, because these are not the responsibility of the county!

Broader understanding and credibility

This really is where you can get a pay-off from being a councillor early in your life, i.e. in your twenties or early thirties. Your experience will lend you authority when applying for senior jobs afterwards. You will get used to dealing with the bureaucratic processes of a council and the experience gained in public speaking will be invaluable. I have many friends who readily admit to only having reached their level of seniority thanks to their early experience of being a councillor.

These senior jobs may be within a council, in a consultancy advising local government, or even at a higher level of government: i.e. as an adviser/researcher to national government. Equally, if you are interested in pursuing a career in national (or European) politics, then a start at local level, while not essential, is certainly very useful.

The Councillor's story

Martin Stott served as a Labour Councillor on Oxford City Council in the 1980s, before going on to become a senior local government officer in the noughties.

> *"At the time I was selected in 1985, I was 31. In the early 1980's political divisions were sharp. Mrs Thatcher had just been re-elected with a huge majority and seen off the Argentinians and, even more traumatically, the miners. Privatisation was in full swing. The Labour Party was in turmoil, with the SDP having split off about three years earlier. Michael Foot had just been replaced by Neil Kinnock*

as leader. Being in the Labour Party and being involved in local government was exciting. The young Ken Livingstone ruled the roost in London and various left leaders were a big deal in local government up and down the country: Derek Hatton in Liverpool, David Blunkett in Sheffield, etc. Local government was seen as the centre of resistance to 'Thatcherism'. She shared this view, abolishing both the GLC and the Met Counties in 1986 and introducing the Poll Tax in Scotland in 1989. Becoming a councillor seemed to be a good way of both supporting my local community in the face of attacks on the social democratic settlement – Neil Kinnock's 'dented shield' – and engaging in those wider debates and campaigns.

Oxford City was quite a radical council. There was an active and organised trade union movement centred around the car factory (it still employed 27,000 people on the Cowley sites as recently as 1981). Combined with the academic / intellectual strand and the flowering of the 'new social movements' (feminism, race, green, gay, etc., which I identified with in my own political practice) it led to a creative mix on the council.

Martin (right) in 1987, with musician Billy Bragg and local MP Andrew Smith (subsequently Minister for Work and Pensions)

In retrospect I was quite lucky. I was immediately on election (May 1986) made Chief Whip – not a very onerous task as Labour had a pretty big majority and the Tories (still the opposition then) were 'wicked'. This was quickly followed by being made Chair of the newly created Economic Development Committee, which very much reflected the times – local government was reaching out into new areas of service delivery and influence (think Alternative Economic Strategies and all that). Because I was young and articulate this rapidly propelled me onto a national stage, joining the Board of the Centre for Local Economic Strategies (CLES) and of 'SEEDS', which was an association of Labour councils in the SE actively attempting to coordinate the implementation of alternative economic strategies in the region. This got me speaking at all kinds of national events.

This had a huge impact on my career because:

a) I engaged in a network of people who were real movers and shakers in local government and economic development nationally;

b) I gained a level of experience and credibility which it would have been difficult to acquire through a conventional 'job';

c) it gave me the opportunity to push through things in Oxford which I'm sure that neither I nor the council would have had the confidence to tackle otherwise. For example, the struggling Old Fire Station was transformed into a successful public/private partnership which is still going over 20 years later. That was my first big project.

Having said all that, being a councillor in those days wasn't paid like it is these days (you got a £20 a day attendance allowance for 'approved meetings', that's all) and by 1988 I had both a small family and a large mortgage. Working part-time for Oxfordshire Co-op Development Agency gave me the flexibility to do council work (and reinforced my credibility in the economic development world) but it wasn't really enough money for my new circumstances.

In 1989 I started to look round for something else and very fortuitously a job came up at Oxfordshire County Council. The new Chief Exec John Harwood had just arrived from

Lewisham Council and had a certain London-radical approach. He created a Chief Executive's Office and Policy Unit to help him manage the council. He looked to recruit a number of dynamic staff to take responsibility for a series of new areas he thought the council ought to be 'players' in, including economic development. I applied for and got the economic development post in 1989. There is absolutely no question that my political experience, track record of delivery and networks in this area made the difference between getting and not getting that job.

There were some real practical issues in the transition from 'member' to 'officer' at that time. I had to resign from Oxford City Council before taking up the post in January 1990 and there was an interesting three months or so when I was kept 'under wraps' and not allowed to speak at committee meetings on my own papers etc. In retrospect this was a very wise move by my managers! After I had passed my probation there was a bit of a debate about my position in the council, as someone who still had a pretty high profile locally. Mrs Thatcher had recently introduced the 'political restriction' rules on local government officers – a reaction basically to 'twin trackers' in London (i.e. people who were councillors in one authority and senior officers in another) and I was immediately promoted to a point where I was 'politically restricted' (this involved about a 20% pay rise!).

I stayed at Oxfordshire for 14 years. In career terms this was not very sensible, but as main carer for two daughters it made a lot of sense to stay. (I worked part-time for 3 years, chaired the council's nursery company, etc.) My knowledge of the local players in the economic development field was incredibly helpful. My track record as a councillor gave me 'name recognition' both in Oxfordshire and beyond and my national contacts enabled Oxfordshire to 'do more' in the economic development field than the resources it deployed would suggest.

> *When I did move to a senior leadership position at Warwickshire County Council in 2004 as Head of Environment and Resources, the combination I had, of 'hands on' delivery, strategic and policy work and empathy with the needs and pressures of elected members, was what got me the job, which needed all those skills and experiences to do it well."*

A first political step

The first thing you will need to do is to join a political party. It is possible to get elected without being a party member but it's certainly not at all easy. You really need to have made something of a name for yourself locally already or a have *a lot* of local friends prepared to help you. There have been some occasions over the last decade of complete unknowns getting elected as mayor, but mayoral contests benefit from local media interest while a single contest in a council ward does not.

Being supported by an existing political party provides access to the organisation necessary to place posters in people's windows, to push leaflets through everyone's doors and to get out the vote on election day. The political party should also be able to underwrite your election expenses.

So which party should you join?

Nowadays there are big overlaps in the three main parties in England – Conservatives, Labour and Liberal Democrats – both in terms of policy and social make-up, so if you want to become an elected councillor, it makes sense to choose the local party that stands most chance of winning. My twenty-year-old self would have shuddered at that sentence because it sounds quite cynical, selfish and 'careerist', but the fact of the matter is that in local government the difference that you can make as an individual is probably more important than the ideology of the party that you choose.

You do need to feel comfortable with the sort of people that make up the active members of the party, though. You will be relying on them to choose you as their candidate and then to put considerable effort into supporting you in your campaign. In this you will gain experience of motivating people and providing leadership. You will receive immediate feedback from:

- party activists who vote with their feet in terms of how much effort they give to support you
- and from voters in how they receive you on the doorstep and whether, on the big day, they turn out and put their cross against your name on the ballot paper.

In some places you may have alternative choices. Where I live, it is generally a contest between the Labour Party and the Green Party, who are a slowly but steadily growing force in English politics, as disillusionment with the main parties sets in. They also possess a more distinctive outlook on the world, which you may feel attracted to if you believe our society really needs some radical change.

Do be conscious of the fact that the party you choose now will shape your future alliances and fortunes if you achieve some prominence as a councillor. It may also affect other people's perceptions of you for years to come.

Your fortunes as a party politician will be partly governed by the popularity of the national party in power. Even in general elections there can be exceptions to this process: for example, Andrew Smith, Labour MP for Oxford East, increased his majority in the 2010 election despite Labour votes falling almost everywhere else in the country. He achieved this in a number of ways:

- ✓ he established a long-standing reputation for being "a good constituency MP", meaning that he always answers letters & emails from his constituents positively when they contact him;
- ✓ he resigned from the Labour Government under Tony Blair to give himself more time to campaign locally before the

election, which also allowed him to distance himself from some of the less popular policies such as the Iraq War;
- ✓ he fostered strong links with the sizeable Pakistani and Bangladeshi communities in Oxford East (for whom British combat against fellow Muslims in Iraq was, of course, widely resented);
- ✓ he has an effective local media presence and supports local industry such as BMW's Mini car plant in Cowley and the local NHS – both sizeable employers.

Another extraordinary exception while I am writing is the by-election victory of George Galloway in Bradford West – for 40 years a safe Labour seat – at a time when opinion polls showed a national increase in Labour support. Galloway succeeded in galvanizing the large local Muslim community, benefitting from both his personal charisma and national notoriety.

Although dyed-in-the-wool tribalism, whereby whole families might pledge lifelong allegiance to a particular party and automatically distrust and disparage anyone coming from an opposing camp, is no longer such a feature of modern politics, the system is still essentially adversarial. One of the things that you will have to accept is that getting yourself elected is a battle against the other candidates. It can be tempting to adopt a cynical approach, speaking up for things just because they are temporarily popular or, conversely, keeping your thoughts quiet for fear they will lose you votes. Equally pernicious can be the temptation to oppose suggestions from other parties just to put them in a bad light – especially if they are being forced by external factors such as budget constraints to make a decision that is unpopular with some outspoken voters.

Another factor that you will have to come to terms with is the organisational processes and bureaucracy, firstly in your own party and then in the council itself, should you be elected. You will inevitably be drawn into a procession of meetings, meetings, and meetings, all mediated by rules, standing orders and procedures. This can actually be useful experience for working in any large organization. You will learn:

- how to operate within given constraints and
- when you can circumvent them or
- get them changed.

Exercise: My personal manifesto

If you are tempted to become a councillor, start by drafting your personal manifesto. It does not matter at this stage which party you would be standing for.

Just write three paragraphs of a few sentences each.

Paragraph 1 – Let me introduce myself

Something about yourself: your background, why you like living in the area where you will be standing for election, your current occupation, your family, your interests. Focus on what will interest local people to read on and consider voting for you.

Paragraph 2 – Why I will be a great councillor

How you will make a difference as a councillor: what are you passionate about that you can influence on the council? What are your values? How will you represent local people's interests?

Paragraph 3 – My track record

If you have already been involved in campaigns or local initiatives, give some details, especially if they were successful. It could include things like organizing local gigs or events. If your experience is limited, then imagine what you might be able to get involved in over the next year and write as if those activities have been achieved.

Being a Councillor

Let's say you choose this option and you are lucky enough to make it – and do bear in mind that this could take a few years of recognised activism in your locality. You usually need to become known and accepted in your local party. Often you have to stand as a candidate in an unwinnable seat before being trusted as the party's standard-bearer in a winnable ward.

You will quickly discover several things which you may find challenging:

a) your main interest might be adult social care, but you will have to deal with many other local issues, the nitty-gritty of people's everyday concerns: rubbish bin collection, rowdy neighbours, planning and highways issues, regeneration and small business regulations. Only about 4% of the total population have any engagement with adult social care at all. This makes the topic electorally relatively unimportant – even though in some councils adult social care spend can be half of the budget. Nevertheless, there will be some issues pertinent to social care, notably benefits and housing – which does mean that in a two-tier authority there is some value in being a District or City Councillor, posts with responsibility for those areas.

b) As a councillor, you will have to engage with people whose circumstances are challenging and difficult. This can be helpful preparation for a career in ASC.

c) Your power to change things quickly will be very limited. There will be an awful lot of wordy reports to digest if you take your role seriously. The council's civil servants (known as 'officers') will write these. They are responsible for the ongoing administration of the council and many of them will outlast the elected councillors. They will have their own views as to how the council should operate, often embedded in standing orders and existing policy. The senior officers who brief councillors have the time and access to resources that members, who are always part-time, do not have. About ten years ago, local government also moved to a 'Cabinet' system. This means that a small group of senior councillors take the major decisions amongst themselves. Each has responsibility for a particular area, just like in the national government. Arguably, this has made local government more efficient than having each topic pondered and debated by a committee, but it does offer ordinary councillors less opportunity for exerting influence. They may be appointed to 'scrutiny committees' where questions can be asked and decisions probed, but these have no real powers.

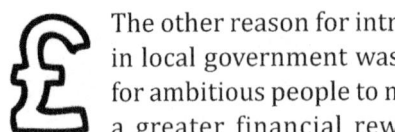

The other reason for introducing the Cabinet system in local government was to make it more attractive for ambitious people to make a difference by offering a greater financial reward for portfolio holders. Cabinet members can earn over £20,000 per annum. If you can combine that with a decent part-time job you can earn a good living, although, given the inevitable time commitments, you are unlikely to grow seriously wealthy.

If you do find local politics interesting, then becoming a Cabinet member would be an extremely useful step on your career ladder. If you choose to take that route, you should look out for a good mentor. Experienced members, or retired members who are still involved in the party, will often be glad of an opportunity to pass on their hard-gained wisdom. You may also receive that kind of support from the Director amongst the civil servants in your department, though this can be a sensitive relationship: whilst you are, technically, their boss, they probably understand the issues in far greater detail than you do and may be many years senior to you, especially if you have entered local politics early in your career.

Finally, one of the benefits that you will enjoy from embarking on local political engagement is that politics attracts 'wannabe' leaders. If your ambition is to make a wider difference in your field, both locally and nationally, it helps greatly to be mixing with other future leaders. It is always a good idea to consider who amongst your network is likely to be in a position of influence in 5 or 10 years' time.

These connections could prove very useful in your future career even if you move out of party politics altogether. They could bring work opportunities as well as personal support.

In a few cases, your early political choices could result in some prejudice against you later on if you are seen to have been closely associated with a particular party ideology, although the decline in political tribalism over the last decades makes this increasingly less likely.

In summary:

Local political leadership may be difficult and under-valued, but it is important.

Furthermore, winning the respect – and the vote! – of your constituents will develop the more specific social care skills described in the next chapter.

Chapter Six

You really need to understand Clients and Carers

Clients and carers are **whole** people. A client or 'service user' or patient is not defined by their disability, illness or frailty. This is just one aspect of their complex life, all of which – their abilities, wants, personal history, family, and social networks – needs to be recognised, understood and supported.

This was always what 'social work' was meant to be about – hence the term. Significant aspects slipped from view after the Community Care Act of 1990 and the trend towards a 'care management' approach by LAs. In recent years the emphasis on personalisation has been an attempt to get back to this approach – although it is always subject to the constraints of time and resources available to LAs (or indeed privately). It's worth noting that the personalisation policy was the result of campaigning by physically disabled people, as well as by groups such as 'In Control', pressing for a better deal for people with learning and other disabilities.

So let's go through some categories of people's needs that you will have to consider in order to be really effective. This could form the subject of a whole book in itself, so I will be very brief.

Physical

At the most basic level people need to eat, drink, sleep and be physically safe and housed. Some forms of care have gone little further than meetings these needs. Yet it is increasingly clear that even people with the most severe medical conditions such as complete paralysis have emotional wants and needs beyond the basic physical ones.

These levels of human needs are often referred to as the Maslow hierarchy of needs. Here's a helpful visual representation of Maslow's theory, categorising human needs in an ascending pyramid.

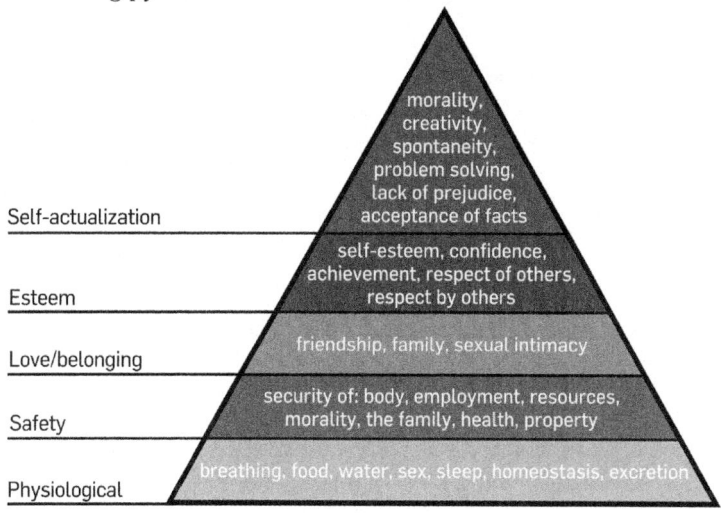

Source: Wikipedia, June 2009. Author: FactoryJoe – used under Creative Commons licence.

Thus, to simplify things slightly, we come next to:

Emotional / social

Emotions are the means by which our human bodies and souls unconsciously know how to take action. We are social beings and need interaction with other people. We need to feel that warm glow which lets us know we have positive connections to the people we value. These could be parents, partners, children, friends, neighbours, or even local shopkeepers.

It's important to bear in mind that social connections may also extend to beloved pets, especially for many single older people. My mother, for example, when she was older and on her own, adopted a stray cat. It had suffered abuse and been in a minor car accident and was, in consequence, rather nervy and unsociable. Nonetheless, she heaped love and affection upon it and it became in time a very friendly and self-assured animal. When my mother went into a hospice at the final stage of her lymphoma, I made a point of taking the cat in to see her. I thought that she might want to see him one last time and say goodbye, as she had been doing with my siblings who lived abroad. As it happened, she wasn't particularly interested in seeing her old pet. In the event it did feel rather inappropriate. We never got round to discussing it. Was she still thinking she would return home? Had she already said her own goodbyes, or had she reached a point where it was only her close family that mattered?

Social services may need to assume responsibility for pets when the owner becomes unable to look after them at home, needs to be admitted to a care home, or passes away.

There is increasing evidence that loneliness itself can lead to significant health problems. According to one research study it could have a similarly deleterious effect on health as smoking 15 cigarettes a day.

Spiritual

At a time of personal trial, many people find profound solace in their spiritual beliefs. True, many of us these days have lost connection to the traditional forms of spirituality offered by the churches. I myself was raised an atheist on the grounds that too many atrocities have been committed over the centuries in the name of organised religions. Science has presented us with major benefits, not least in terms of improved physical wellbeing, reduced infant and perinatal mortality and longer life expectancy. Scientific method has no interest in the existence of God and unflinchingly challenges many truth claims derived from scriptural authority. Nevertheless, as I get older, I increasingly recognise the attractions of spirituality and the belief in a power greater than humanity. It's fine with me if some people choose to call that power 'God'.

Whatever your personal views, it is scientifically true that we humans have an inbuilt tendency towards belief in a higher spirit. A friend of mine works with refugees who have undergone traumatic upheaval and dislocation. She has observed how it is the ones with the strongest religious beliefs who are best able to cope with their experiences and rebuild their lives. When we are faced with a crisis that profoundly challenges our sense of self and the purpose of our life here on earth, we need something more than extended shopping opportunities and the distractions of television. Especially at the end of their lives, people's spiritual needs deserve to be deeply respected.

Spirituality can take many forms beyond the traditional forms located in churches, mosques, synagogues and temples, with their rituals conducted by professional representatives or interpreters of the divine will – vicars, priests, rabbis, imams, etc. For some people, spirituality is something encountered through immersion in nature. For others, it may be a matter of pursuing a deep connection to their ancestors, both immediate and those distant in time.

Those are my various categories of needs. You should take them all into account throughout your career when dealing with people in need of care and support.

My next advice in this chapter is to

Listen to stories of clients and carers

Yes, I will use the term 'client' as I cannot come up with a single better word. You will soon realise in the world of social care that some people are extremely particular about their use of words. Some may object to the word 'client' because it implies a dependency on the professional. 'Service user' has achieved some widespread currency, but to me this sounds too much like bureaucratic jargon.

Anyway, listen to them in their own words.

I will just give you one story here, which I've found very moving and which I was given through my work supporting people with dementia and especially their carers.

This is the story of Meg Barbour, a remarkable lady. Her husband was diagnosed with dementia. Thanks to her determination to give something back for the support that she received, she has become a significant local leader of carers, setting up and supporting local groups.

"This is my personal experience of caring for my husband. He suffered from Lewy Body Dementia over a period of some six or seven years. This is a less common form of dementia than Alzheimer's, but presents itself in a very similar way, and can really only be confirmed after death. First I will tell you a little about us, so that you will better understand this sad journey that we took together.

Just over forty years ago I met this lovely man, an Edinburgh man, eleven years older than me, who wanted me to be his wife. We were just so good together and we knew it was right, so we married in my church in Hertfordshire on my 23rd birthday, in front of our families and asking God to bless our union. We set off on the sea of life in our little boat, confidently sailing out into the ocean, enjoying our freedom, the stars and each other's company. My man was the captain, and I was, well, everything else really. In time God sent us four new little sailors and we hugged the shore for a while so that the boat would be relatively steady as they grew. The little sailors became strong and were able to help the Captain, so we ventured out into unknown waters, and they were at times calm and at other times choppy, but it was fun and looking back now it was our finest of times . . . You know what comes next: the little sailors, now bigger than us, join other boats and sail off to other seas, with our blessing, of course, and suddenly we have seen 30 years pass by and we are again sailing our own boat . . . just us alone. Yippee!

Looking back now, 1996 was a very good year for us; at the time I didn't realise how good. In June that year my husband Ced retired from his Finance post in the University and ten days later on my 53rd birthday we celebrated our 30th wedding anniversary by going on holiday to Scotland with two of our four children. He was full of his usual playful antics, teasing me about my preoccupation with the splendid Aga we found in our rented house, something I'd always wanted in my kitchen; playing ball with the dogs, and just so relaxed at the start of his retirement. To mark the event he grew a beard, knowing he no longer had to be clean-shaven for work. We both looked forward to some special time on our own. 'Let's do all the things we promised ourselves, and were never free to do,' said the Captain, and we started to plan like a couple of schoolkids.

Over the next few months I became aware that something was amiss. Being in each other's company most of the day let me see that although his vocabulary was as good as ever, words sometimes came out wrong or in the wrong context, and his writing was becoming spidery and untidy, quite unlike what I was used to. He couldn't see there was anything wrong, but to placate me he agreed to visit his GP. We were referred to a memory Assessment Clinic in May 1997. In July, as kindly as he could, the Doctor diagnosed suspected Alzheimer's disease.

I was devastated and anxious to learn all I could about what this meant for us both. Ced just thought it was nonsense and a big mistake.

It was suggested that I get in touch with the Alzheimer's Society. I found the Oxfordshire branch in my home village of Wheatley, and discovered I knew several members. They kindly and gently answered my panicky questions about what the future might hold for us and advised me to see my lawyer and investigate an enduring power of attorney. Sterling advice as it turned out, but the first of many awkward things I had to tackle. Ced meanwhile thought none of this applied to him. He used to read The Telegraph cover to cover and he cut out all articles that contained the dreaded 'A' word. At this time I remember asking someone from the A.S.: 'If I look after him, keep him warm and make sure he eats good food and love him like always, why will he die?' As gently as he could, he told me that we might have many years together but the brain controls every part of our bodies and when ultimately his brain dies, then his body will stop working too.

Around this time I had a small but hair-raising journey to the supermarket with Ced driving me in Archie, his white Morris Minor. Up till then I had felt that although he was rather slow, to say the least, he was safe to drive, and taking me to shop just down the road was good for his self-esteem and gave him a feeling of having achieved something. He drove out in front of a bus, believing I'm sure that he had the right of way, when he really hadn't. He was frightened and so was I. He soon forgot but I could not afford to and had to see his GP and write to the DVLA. He was desperately upset when the driving license was withdrawn and sat down to write to his MP. It kept him occupied for two or three days on and off, and at the end he just gave me a very shaky and ill-written copy of the letter he had received from his GP telling him he was no longer allowed to drive. It was all written in a wandering shaky hand, misspelt and almost illegible. I promised to post it, felt like a Judas for betraying him, went down the garden into the shed, curled up in the corner and cried.

My poor dear man was sick and was not going to get better. He couldn't be Captain any more. I had to do that and, in time, everything else too. This was the point when I clumsily brought the old boat to shore and we stepped off, to walk hand in hand, and a dreadful tug of war began. I was on one side, he was in the middle and the relentless beast of Alzheimer's was on the other. I wasn't used to being at the helm and I floundered a lot and made a lot of mistakes, and the very nature of his illness meant that he wasn't able to help me much.

I was quite frightened now, and knew with certainty that I needed help. He was gentle, quiet but lacking in any drive or initative. This was no longer a partnership, I was on my own.

A visit to his GP got us a referral to a Community Psychiatric Nurse (CPN), who then visited me regularly. She helped me to accept the fact that I was going to need day care, and unlike me, was quite confident that Ced would accept this. 'I've never had a failure yet', she said confidently, and I secretly thought 'Please God, don't let this be your first'. She arranged for him to go to Wykeham Park day hospital in Thame on a Friday and to share a taxi with another patient going there. He was not happy and for the first time I lied to him and told him he was going to help with research. He had been a university student in Edinburgh in his youth, had then worked for Oxford University for many years and had a high regard for the value of research. So he agreed somewhat grudgingly, muttering that he had no idea how he could be of interest to anyone. It was still a little difficult at first but soon became routine. He would take a small book containing my written account of things we had done in the last week and he would bring back the Occupational Therapist's account of his day. This Friday was so precious for me, a chance for me to be off duty. I knew he was safe and well cared for and I could relax.

Helen, our only daughter, decided to travel to New Zealand to meet the family of her fiancé, and while there to marry so that all his family could be there and involved. 'Wonderful idea', I said. 'We can have a blessing here in our church when you come home.' As time went on and she phoned to tell me about flowers and dresses and hymns, I went a bit wobbly and realised I REALLY wanted to be there. 'Go', said our boys. 'We'll look after Dad.' I was dubious about that as they all lived in different parts of the country and did not know how difficult things were for him. I had to tell him what I wanted to do and when I did, he looked so worried and crestfallen, I asked if he wanted to come and he made me understand that he did. So we went on our great adventure of discovery and loneliness. We discovered that people were not at all aware of our problems and just did not understand when he failed to ask for things. We discovered the toilets on aircraft are made only for single occupancy, and I found true desolation on the other side of the world. Helen was ecstatic to see us as she had no idea we were coming and cried tears of happiness as her father took his only daughter down the aisle. After the wedding, they returned to the UK, but we could not get back for another week. We were in a motel in windy Wellington, knew hardly anyone and Ced was frightened every time we ventured out. Then I knew how much support I had from my church, other friends and family . . . at home.

The CPN also suggested that we might now benefit from a weekly visit from a 'flexible carer' supplied by Age Concern and I leapt at the chance of an hour a week to take the dogs for a brisk walk or go to the shops alone. Ced's walking was now very slow and he held my hand like a small child. We were so lucky to meet a gentle caring lady who came one hour a week to keep him company or take him for a drive or a slow wander. She stayed with us for a year and a half and was able to see weekly his changes and advise and support me at review meetings. She made me realise that getting him upstairs to bed at night was becoming a danger; she introduced him to a daycentre run again by Age Concern, in Thame. She took him the first time and he went each Wednesday for over a year. We made new friends but sadly had to lose our flexible carer as Ced became more unaware. We understood that lots of others needed to benefit from this wonderful service. So the flexible care went out and incontinence came in. Pads, special pants and sheets and the occasional accident became a fact of life.

During this time the CPN arranged for a visit from Social Services. I imagine we were put on file somewhere, as the lady visitor sympathetically asked questions, observed the health of my husband, assured herself that he had more than £20,000 in funds and then disappeared. I would like to think that the visit from the O.T. from Abingdon who arranged for a handrail to be put over the bath, and for us to borrow a toilet frame and seat, came from the social worker's visit but I just don't know.

Everyone told me I needed a holiday and I should have respite care for my husband. I was so unhappy to place him somewhere for a week where he had never been before, and my ideal would have been for him to stay at Wykeham Park where he was known and felt happy but this was not possible as it was only a DAY hospital. So I looked around for a day centre that could also offer respite care at a later date. I didn't realise then that I was looking for Gold Dust. At last I found one at Cumnor and I paid for Ced to go to this homely, friendly place where he spent some time on Tuesdays. He was collected at 10am and returned at about 4 and I knew that as soon as he was comfortable I could think about having a break. His week was now quite varied and apart from getting him ready for his transport in the morning, I had quite a few windows in my days to do things.

Now came another ray of light into this world of caring: the Alzheimer's Society appointed a 'carers support worker'. At last someone for me!!!! She was and still is a lifeline. She can't do the impossible but she listens and suggests and is there. She brought me into a new carers support group that she was starting on Fridays in Manzil Way, Oxford, with Age Concern. The support I have been given by all who attend there is immeasurable. I still go and now help run a lunch club for sufferers and carers myself. The Isis carers support group has done great things for me and lots of others, but more about this later.

I asked the home at Cumnor for a week's respite for Ced and spent the week worrying that he was all right. Of course he was. He came home as if he had been in the garden for a few hours. This made me more confident to ask them to collect him from the church in Leamington Spa and keep him overnight when one of our sons married, so that I could be free to enjoy the reception. Sounds so logical and such a good idea as I say it now, but how heart-wrenching it was to encourage him into a car and watch him being driven off, when I had always imagined he would be by my side at these special family times.

Normally he was loving and gentle and quite pleased to accommodate my wishes, and me, but occasionally he would have an infection and then he changed. He pushed me away, saw things that weren't there and became very agitated and less able to do anything. About now I hit my all time low. One Sunday afternoon, he was unwell, distant and agitated and I felt unable to reach him at all. He made me under-

stand that he wanted the toilet. I got him up, my shoulder under his armpit and we started down the hall; suddenly he stopped as if his batteries had run out, he could go neither forward nor back and his legs started to give way, we were alone in the house and I was really afraid. I grabbed a chair and stuck it under him and fetched one for myself, and we both sat side by side in our hall. I hugged him for an hour while two paracetemol tablets took effect and watched while a wet stain spread across his lap. I phoned our GP and got a duty doctor who told me to dial 999 if I needed help. I really didn't need an ambulance, just a strong arm to help Ced and a friendly shoulder for me to cry on; at that moment I was the only person on an alien planet.

As he was becoming almost unaware of his surroundings and asleep a lot of the time he was getting next to nothing from his visits to Wykeham Park and so this was withdrawn. Just when I had got to my most difficult time on a caring road, help was leaving me. I had to put a bed downstairs and we now slept apart. I had left him even in sleep but of course he did not know. The Carers Centre helped me purchase a pressure mat that would alert me upstairs if he got out of bed downstairs and I had some help from Crossroads to wash and dress him in the mornings and toilet him. Dr. Jane Pearce, his specialist, gently suggested it was time to look for a nursing home and asked why didn't I consider the one in my own village? I did and they were very kind and considerate. After viewing five others, I decided that placing him somewhere near to me really was easier than far away. After a very sad and difficult family Xmas, one of my sons and his wife helped me take him there on 28th December 2002. As I helped him over the threshold I felt like a complete betrayer. I knew in my heart that he would never walk out of there and that I could and would. My work as a full time carer ended that day and reluctantly I just had to accept that I was no longer able to give him the care he needed.

I hope he knew that I still cared for him so much, even though I was no longer caring for him at home and I had physically left him in the main in the care of others. I visited very often and my friends did too, I bathed him and sang to him and hugged him, but he was almost gone now.

I was awarded a few little glimpses of my dear man on a random occasional basis and he stayed in the nursing home until his death on 26th July 2004. It was the end of an onerous journey for us both and for our children. The church was full as we asked God to keep him safely for us and as always the warmth of support from my church family was there.

All through this time and after, I had the support of my family, three sons and a daughter and three grandchildren who he really did not know at all. And beyond them was my church family, watching and feeling for my distress. I have always considered my friends in the congregation of St. Mary's in Wheatley as part of my extended family and their support was so valuable. Close family are so involved emotionally, that talking with them sometimes just increases the hurt and anxiety because they feel for not just one parent but two. Anyway, neither their father nor I would have wanted their lives blighted by this illness any more than it had to be. I tried to keep them out of it as much as I could, as I knew this would have been his wish. He was a great Dad, ran Saturday morning Football and a Cub Pack for many years, took Helen to ballet each and every week and gave up his own pursuits to be around them. His own father had not taken an interest in him, being much more interested in alcohol, and this had determined him to be different. The children's own journey through this was a sad one but a whole new story, and different for each.

The role of a carer in this disease is a lonely one; there are times you feel trapped and isolated: trapped because you are unable to leave the person you care for alone, and isolated because they maybe do not speak and appear to be sometimes someone completely unknown to you. What a cruel blow... There is a role here for kindly mental support, an ear that does not hasten away or eyes that hold yours and do not look away. An offer of a visit to stay and have a cup of tea with the person you care for, so that you can grab the dog and feel the wind on your face for a while. It is not rocket science and costs nothing except time. I found this in my church and still do. God supported me through all this and gave me support through others too. He gave me little windows of peace along the road and although going to church was a little more difficult than it had been because of having to dress him and get him there, it was always a refreshing experience for me; for him I really do not know... We attended a home communion one Easter in the house of two dear ladies who fussed over him with great sincerity of feeling, and although at that time he was saying very little of any sense, when we were all invited to say a prayer he, out of the blue said a few words to God which made perfect sense and we all felt the tears start."

For me this story illustrates many different aspects of social care and I will refer back to some of these as we progress through the rest of the book.

As Meg herself will always remind people, it is only one story and everyone's story is different. If you are going to work across the board in ASC, then make sure you keep listening to stories of different client groups (e.g. Learning Disabilities, Mental Health, Physical Disabilities, as well as Older People) and from different ages of clients and carers. You will notice both significant generational differences as well as broad similarities in the fundamentals.

People do not always want to be helped

This is an important one to remember. In Meg's story, the 'client', her husband, did not accept that he had a problem. This can be the case in many circumstances, not just with dementia.

Frequently, people will not realize that their condition is having an adverse affect on other people – usually partners or other family members – and that this warrants outside support.

Many people just don't want interference from strangers. They may fear losing control of their destiny. For example, if they are approaching the end of their life, they may be determined to spend their last years, months, weeks or days in their own home and be afraid of being taken to a home or a hospital.

Some people are more private than others and may feel shame in accepting outside support. There may be well-founded fears of engaging with 'officialdom', associating local authority social services with other aspects of the state such as the police. This can be a particular issue if there are mental health problems or drug and alcohol complications. There may be financial reasons why people are protective of their privacy.

Clearly, it is generally important to respect people's wishes if they do not want support, or only a limited and specific element of support. There may, however, be some occasions when it is justifiable to step beyond this if there are risks to the individual or those around them. This is a sensitive moral and legal topic, requiring specialist, experienced advice.

Sometimes, people will simply benefit from being offered more than they realised was available. I attended a home assessment with an occupational therapist for an elderly man with mobility problems who was being looked after by his retired daughter and his son. It was clear that they had always been proudly self-sufficient but just wanted the local authority to help with the cost of installing a stairlift. The OT was able to survey the house further and give some tips about grab rails and risks of slipping on rugs, etc.

Remember: you can walk away from their lives, but they cannot.

 You will be seen as an expert or an authority figure, but only on the aspect of their lives where support is needed. In many cases, just one word or sentence from you can have a significant impact – you will be shifting the parameters of what is possible for the client.

There are numerous anecdotes of how Personal Budgets, in facilitating small changes in people's support services, have rendered them huge benefits, and at no additional cost to the LA. For example, there was the case of an elderly lady who was receiving regular transport assistance to attend her local LA day centre. As far as the social worker was concerned this met her identified need for social contact, but when she was asked what was really important to her, she revealed that she had not seen her sister for years even though she only lived 20 miles away. Her Personal Budget was able to pay for the taxi to visit her sister instead of some of the day centre visits.

The Age UK Support Brokerage service, funded by Oxfordshire County Council, has many such stories. Two that stick in my mind concern men with mobility problems who were enabled through using their Personal Budgets to get occasional support to indulge their lifelong passions, respectively angling and sailing. No doubt these were desires that would previously not have been shared with a social worker; they would not have been deemed feasible under a traditional approach to service delivery.

Of course, there will always be concerns not shared with you – often their deepest wishes, fears or fantasies. Sometimes it can be regarding sexual desires: this is a topic that could form the subject of moral (and legal) debate about what it is acceptable to spend a Personal Budget on. Around the corner from where I live is one of the world's first hospices for children. They had a late-teenaged boy with a terminal illness in their care who expressed the wish for sexual experience. After some discussion, of course including his parents, it was agreed to arrange for a sex worker to visit him at the hospice, which was generally considered a very positive step (and was the subject of a television programme).

There are many ways to keep in touch with client concerns.

If you find yourself climbing up the career ladder into higher levels of management, you will find your direct interaction with clients being reduced. There are various good ways by which you can stay in contact with the viewpoint of 'service users', whether you are working in a local authority, a sizeable private care provider or in central government.

- **'Service User' groups**: these are organising forums for people using particular services to get together and share their experiences with one other. They can also deliver feedback to service providers (which, if it is challenging, may be all the more valuable), as well as offering you, as provider, a degree of public recognition, should this be an important consideration for you.

- **User-Led Organisations (ULOs)**: in recent years the Department of Health has increasingly been encouraging local authorities to engage with or set these up. This originated under the Labour Government but also fits perfectly with Big Society concepts. Because they require voluntary commitment from the very people who are in need of support, these can be difficult to sustain across all client groups on a representative and ongoing basis but, where they do operate, they can be very effective. In some places there are disabled people's campaign groups which have been active for many years. These tend to be primarily for physically disabled people, who form a relatively small proportion of a council's social care clients.

- **One-to-one meetings and visits** to individuals in their homes, to care homes, to day centres, etc. Simply talking directly, one-to-one, without it being a formal assessment or interview, can be very informative. I remember being struck by the approach of one Assistant Director on a county council. He was having to review the county's policy on providing cheap transport to take elderly people to day centres. There was a proposal to limit the transport only to those individuals whose need was so great that the council had a legal duty to assist them. His background was finance and management rather than social work and he could have approached it as a paper-based exercise. Instead, he made a point of going out travelling on one of the minibuses which pick people up from rural areas and talking to the passengers. It became apparent to him just how much they valued the service for keeping them active and meeting people. For many who were not legally eligible for council support it was what kept them going. Without it they would be more likely to deteriorate and then need council services. Only in this way could he fully appreciate the preventative nature of the service and how cutting it might incur higher costs than would be saved.

- **Research and publications**: there is a growing body of research into people's experiences, notably from Demos, the Social Care Institute for Excellence (SCIE) and the King's Fund. It can also, where appropriate, be commissioned, should you, as a leader, have access to the necessary resources. There are numerous online publications, such as Community Care (*www.communitycare.co.uk*), which carry stories about service users and carers, as well as lobby groups such as Carers UK, Age UK, the Alzheimer's Society, etc.

Seek out clients' and carers' experiences even before you start your ASC career

Try volunteering in a local care home, working with people with learning disability or alongside a local charity, for example if they offer a care brokerage service.

Exercise: Gathering Client and Carer stories

Set yourself a target of gathering three client or carer stories over the next one to three weeks. This could be from people you know personally, either those in need of care and support or those providing it. Alternatively, you could tell the story of someone you've known in the past.

Write up each story in words and with pictures. Make them as long or short as you like. I've left some blank pages for you.

Highlight what you think are the main points.

❊ ❊ ❊ ❊ ❊ ❊ ❊ ❊

Client or Carer Story # 1

Name:

Situation now:

Story:

What was it that really mattered to this person?

Client or Carer Story # 2

Name:

Situation now:

Story:

What was it that really mattered to this person?

Client or Carer Story # 3

Name:

Situation now:

Story:

What was it that really mattered to this person?

Make carers your allies!

Over the last 15 years, the important role of informal carers has been increasingly recognised, not least due to the lobbying efforts of groups like Carers UK. LAs have also come to appreciate that if carers are not supported, then they become unable to cope and will require a greater (and correspondingly more expensive) level of support from the LA.

Do be wary of carers growing resentful at being drawn into bureaucratic entanglements or being considered a 'free' resource.

Personal Budgets have opened up some opportunities for family members and friends to receive a degree of financial recompense for care that they provide. The rules on this are, however, very clear, and do not extend to family members in the same household receiving payment from the Personal Budget for care delivered.

In some respects and with some clients, the social worker can take on the role of a 'life coach'. For example, the support planning process is very much about identifying what really matters in a person's life and coming up with creative ways of meeting their wider wishes as well as their more direct needs. This can sometimes include helping the person to change their way of thinking about their life, either finding a way to empower themselves more and take more risks (something explicitly encouraged in early Personal Budget pilots) or learning to accept the constraints of their circumstances and make the best they can out of them.

There is a view that a market is opening up for people to offer this sort of service privately as independent support assistants – not just for people who can afford their own care but, potentially, for clients to spend a small amount of their Personal Budget on.

Chapter Seven

"No-one goes into Social Work to become a DASS"

Those are the words of Terry Dafter, Director of Adult Social Services ('DASS') at Stockport Metropolitan Borough Council. "So why did you get into social work?" I asked him.

He started by recalling being in his final year at university, his social sciences course nearly completed, and discussing his options with the career adviser. Terry explained how he wanted to work with people... "maybe something like a social worker". At that time you would normally have needed some experience in the field to be accepted onto a CQSW course (Certificate of Qualification in Social Work – see note below). By chance, the careers adviser was aware of a new MA course at the University of the East of England in Norwich that was accepting postgraduates without experience to study for a CQSW. So that was the fortuitous reason why Terry started his career in social care.

It did not take much prompting for Terry to share the deeper, much more personal motivation:

> *"My mum had a very difficult psychiatric condition. She was sectioned frequently throughout her life – often in front of me. She was very poorly – what we'd call a bi-polar condition now. You could say I had a difficult childhood. Sometimes I'd come home and all the curtains would be drawn and my mum would have been sat in the back room crying all day.*
>
> *Or she'd be high as a kite running round the house at two in the morning doing the cleaning or lighting a bonfire in the garden.*
>
> *I went into generic social work at first because that's what everyone did in those days. I joined an intake team in Manchester social services. We were chucked in at the deep end then and had to rely on peer support. I sectioned someone on my first day and took kids into care in my second week. I like to think we nurture our new social workers a little more these days!*
>
> *It's not surprising that I moved into a mental health role fairly quickly. Manchester saw the need for specialists and the 1983 Mental Health Act was coming into effect with the Approved Social Worker responsibility. I found it interesting to work with families where the parent was ill with a mental health condition and then help consider what to do about the children. I could relate to that."*

I responded by saying I could fully understand his situation, having had some limited experience of the bi-polar condition myself.

Social worker qualifications in the UK

The main qualification for social work is the undergraduate bachelor's degree (BA, BSc or BSW) in social work, offered at British universities from September 2003 onwards. There is also a master's degree (MA, MSc or MSW) available. These have replaced

> the previous qualifying award, the postgraduate Diploma in Social Work (DipSW), which was first awarded in 1991, to be phased out across the UK by 2009. Prior to this, the recognised qualification was the Certificate of Qualification in Social Work (CQSW), awarded between 1975 and 1991.
>
> Purporting to be either a social worker or a student social worker without registering with the Social Work Register and holding or undergoing training for the recognised qualifications is now a criminal offence. Social workers must renew their registration every three years. These regulations offer protection to vulnerable people by guaranteeing the professional regulation of people working as social workers. They also promote workforce development, as all social workers must participate in at least fifteen days of professional training over a three-year period in order to be eligible for renewal of their registration.
>
> Lay practitioners in the United Kingdom, often referred to as Social Services Assistants or Care Workers, are unregistered social workers who often do not hold any formal social work qualification. This is not the case in Scotland where the scope of registration for social service workers is more advanced. Within the mental health sector in the United Kingdom, social workers can train as an Approved Mental Health Professional. With the implementation of the Mental Health Act 2007, this had replaced the previous Approved Social Worker role and is open to other professionals such as community psychiatric nurses, psychologists and occupational therapists, whilst maintaining a social work ethos. AMHPs are responsible for organising and contributing to assessments under the Mental Health Act 1983, as amended by the Mental Health Act 2007.
>
> *(Source: http://en.wikipedia.org/wiki/Qualifications_for_professional_social_work)*

Here is another account of someone's route into social work, eventually leading to his becoming the DASS of the largest local authority in the United Kingdom. The words are from Drew Clode's interview with Peter Hay, DASS at Birmingham and in

2012 President of the Association for Directors of Adult Social Services, a role that regularly took him to No 10 Downing Street and Whitehall.

> Two grandmothers predominated: one a volunteer in a local hospital well into her eighties, the other a teacher for as long and who, having been made redundant during the 1980s, carried on doing almost exactly what she'd done before on a voluntary basis . . .
>
> Add to this parents who were 'deeply rooted' in supporting their local village church in the rural Cambridgeshire of the 1980s and '90s – his mother was also a volunteer for Cruse, providing support to bereaved people - and there can be no surprise that even during his school holidays Peter was volunteering to help run breaks for children from mixed backgrounds. Nor that, by the time he'd left University, the volunteer bug had bitten harder, and he had spent time teaching literacy skills to youngsters of his own age on a voluntary basis and set up a project aided by lottery money and the Children's Society.
>
> This was dedicated to providing weekends away for challenging adolescents in order to provide respite for hard-pressed parents. ('I strongly remember meeting kids who'd never seen a banana', he says.) The project still survives in his alma mater city of Swansea, although far removed from the run-down docks area where it had been born. It was work he was to continue in Northern Ireland, from as early as 1985, working with mixed Catholic and Protestant children. It was ultimately to lead to his meeting Carmel, whom he was to marry in 1989.
>
> *(reproduced from the ADASS newsletter 'ADASS Futures', October 2011, with thanks to Peter and Drew)*

OK, so we've had a couple of examples of what led these future leaders to enter social care, but what drove their progression to become DASSs? What are the factors that might motivate **you** to become a DASS?

The first one you might think of is **Money**.

This is often the reason given why people strive to clamber up the career ladder and it's not a bad one – we all want to do better for ourselves financially if we can, to treat ourselves, to take a much-needed holiday, perhaps to be able to afford a family. Never forget, though, that money should **only ever** be a tool for gaining other satisfactions, not an end in itself.

As a DASS you will manage many staff and be responsible for a substantial budget. Increasingly in our society, even in the public sector, this means earning a significantly larger income than the average. But it won't be the main motivator for someone to become a DASS in ASC. Indeed, if you allow it to drive you, there is a real risk that you will be promoted up to the level of your incompetence, which will over time lead to thoroughgoing unhappiness and perhaps even culminate in a breakdown. Promotion to the level of people's incompetence is a significant, documented risk in rigid hierarchical organisations, known as the Peter Principle. (Peter, Laurence J & Hull, Raymond, *The Peter Principle: Why Things Always Go Wrong*. William Morrow and Company, New York, 1969)

For Terry and many other DASSs the reason for aiming for the top is a combination of the personal challenge and the intellectual challenge.

Here are his own words:

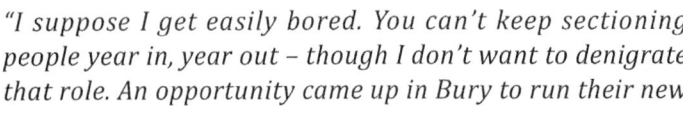

"I suppose I get easily bored. You can't keep sectioning people year in, year out – though I don't want to denigrate that role. An opportunity came up in Bury to run their new

"No-one goes into Social Work to become a DASS"

Community Mental Health Team. The emphasis was now on finding ways of keeping people with mental health problems at home. It was a multi-disciplinary team with nurses and psychiatrists and intellectually challenging. It was something different.

After Manchester with its teaching hospitals and resources, moving to a small authority like Bury was a shock. We had to fight for resources for mental health and sometimes fight with the psychiatrists. It was a very medicalised model of care then – 'pump them full of largactil and they will be all right' – poor souls!

Then Bury re-organised, as local government regularly does, and they created the role of Area Manager with responsibility across all adult social care services: Learning Disability, Older People, Mental Health. I enjoyed the variety of this role. I ran one LD hostel and two old people's care homes amongst the other responsibilities. This was another intellectual challenge and a people skills one as well, managing the performance levels of staff.

I spent 18 years at Bury. The Community Care Act came into effect while I was there in a senior management role. This required new skills again: working with the independent sector and negotiating contracts, formal assessments, introducing a performance regime for the national local government Performance Assessment Framework (PAF).

In 2000 Stockport Council introduced the post of Assistant Director for Strategy and Performance, so my PAF work stood me in good stead when I applied. Stockport Social Services was a woolly, cuddly sort of place at the time where no-one was 'counting beans'. We just assumed that, because we were well-intentioned social workers, what we were doing was effective. Now we needed to establish measures to assess that what we were doing was working. This was completely alien to social work at that time!

My university training in social sciences and statistics helped. I implemented processes in our CareFirst computer system to measure things and extract the management information.

You know, to be honest, in my whole career I'd struggle to recall managers who inspired me. I learned a lot from many examples of bad management. Especially in those days, people would get promoted to a management role because they were good social workers and then find management difficult. In fact, it is still a problem to find the good leaders (as opposed to managers) that we need now to implement Personalisation fully. I have a great senior management team but we can still improve the career path and development lower down the scale.

Six months after I joined Stockport Council, we had a new Director of Social Services, Jean Daintith, who was an inspiring leader. She was driven, focused and cared passionately about Stockport becoming known as amongst the best performers and somewhere to be proud of. She would say to her team: 'You are senior managers. You can make a difference. What do you want to be remembered for?'

When she had to relocate to London for personal reasons, it was a natural progression for me to take on her DASS role in 2009.

So what would I say to someone interested in working in adult social care? Well, if you are going to work in local government, it's where the action is! It's different and innovative because we have to be. We have led the way on personalisation of public services.

Serve your time for a bit but question and don't take everything as read. See what is working well and what isn't. If you have the passion to change something, then don't sit there and blame us but do something about it. It's a really exciting time to work in adult social care. "

"No-one goes into Social Work to become a DASS"

Terry's account neatly illustrates the typical steps along the way to becoming a DASS:

- ✔ a local team leader
- ✔ an area manager
- ✔ experience across multiple client groups
- ✔ operational delivery experience
- ✔ commissioning and contracting experience dealing with the private sector
- ✔ being an Assistant Director
- ✔ shifts between employers at key points
- ✔ responding effectively to changes in legislation.

There is also, of course, a degree of luck, but people can make their own luck. All that luck can do is offer up opportunities; it's up to you to take them.

In the interview cited earlier, Peter Hay stressed the importance of good teachers and role models and the willingness to seek them out.

> In his last two university placements he remembers 'absolutely fantastic' practice teachers who helped him emerge at the age of 23 with, in many ways, the world of social work as his oyster. The pearl he chose was Grimsby, largely because of the innovative neighbourhood focus being pioneered there by director David Peryer, and an inspiring team manager called Margaret Dennison. Peter was clear that he wanted good team management and good supervision, benefits gained from both these colleagues in spades . . .

In a little while, I will talk about all the reasons why people do NOT go into social work to become a DASS, and then discuss some key aspects of the role, but first let's focus on the final motivator: for most DASSs I would say this is not a conscious starting point at all but a factor that slowly and increasingly brings its own reward.

Public Recognition

As DASS you will be known by a large number of staff: there may be anything between 1,000 and 10,000 working for the council, and many of these will be reporting ultimately to you! You will also be known to scores of service and materials providers, whose staff will be keen to sell to your department. Your name will be familiar to thousands of clients and their carers, and many hundreds of them will meet or at least see you personally at presentations. You will be known to thousands of interested members of the public through the local media and may also occasionally be featured in the national media.

Here is where we come to the big downside of public recognition. In most cases, as a DASS you will only come to the public's wider attention when something goes wrong in your patch, on your watch. This used to be a much bigger concern when Directors of Social Services (DSSs) had responsibility for Child Protection as well as adult social care. But there can also be instances of abuse or malpractice in ASC: in the last few years many such cases have been in the headlines, such as the abuses perpetrated at the Winterbourne View home for people with Learning Disabilities.

Of course, if you do crave public recognition, then there are more high profile roles that you can progress to beyond being a DASS. Within a Council some DASSs go on to become Chief Executives (for example, Peter Gilroy at Kent County Council, who was earning £220,000 per annum and notoriously received a further £200,000 as severance payment when he left the council). Anthony Douglas, who was Director of Social Services (DSS) at London Borough of Havering, went on to take up the challenge of managing Cafcass, the Children and Family Court Advisory and Support Service. Cafcass officers interview children and parents in divorce and child contact court cases and write up their recommendations for the judge.

Quite a few DASSs move on to advisory roles within Whitehall or in quangos. For example, the widely respected Julie Jones, who was DSS at Westminster City Council, was Chief Executive of the Social Care Institute for Excellence (SCIE) for 5 years. SCIE provides valued best practice guidance to staff and organisations right across the sector. Robert Lake, formerly DSS at Staffordshire, became Director for Social Care at the NHS Information Centre ('the authoritative source of information about health and social care'). Others who have moved into top Whitehall jobs or gone self-employed as advisers to and managers for Government include David Behan, John Bolton, Jeff Jerome and Glen Mason.

Another career progression from being a DASS can be moving to the private sector. Julia Ross, for example, was Director of Social Services at Barking & Dagenham and became Chief Executive of the Primary Care Trust there as well (a combined role which was something of a stretch). She then had a spell at the Department of Health and went on to become Managing Director for Care & Health Trak and is now Chief Operating Officer for PI Benchmark, owner of the Care & Health Trak products. This move into the commercial world after a lifetime spent in the public sector is likely to require some sort of cultural re-orientation.

Someone who has made that adjustment seamlessly is Stephen Sloss: he has succeeded in transferring the public service values developed in his tenure as DASS of Blackburn With Darwen to his independent agency Salvere, a social enterprise delivering Support Assistants.

I will come back to the links between ASC, social enterprises and the commercial world in Chapter Ten, where we will hear more from Stephen.

First, though, I'd like to explore the flipside of Public Recognition, perhaps more attractive to those taking on on a leadership role in ASC because it connects up with Heart and Brain.

Influence

As a DASS you are in a position to leave a legacy of lasting benefit if you are successful in influencing things at three levels:

1) within your department: your staff and external partners, your clients and their carers
2) corporately across the council and your locality, as part of the executive management team;
3) nationally, by promoting changes to policy and practice, e.g. through the Association of Directors of Adult Social Services.

The first almost goes without saying. A lot will depend on the state of the department when you take over. If it has been performing badly, then there is an opportunity for you to make a significant impact, but this will demand real energy, determination and a supportive management team around you. If the department that you have been asked to manage is already a well-oiled machine, this will allow more possibility for delegation, leaving you with more time to focus on the wider perspectives. Nonetheless, your own department must always come first and will always require your attention as policy, personnel and circumstances change.

For many DASSs, engagement with the wider council is less important. ASC is generally the largest department within a council in terms of both budget and staff, so DASSs can be excused from the broader council responsibilities faced by other LA Directors. On the other hand, there will be areas of the council which do directly impact on ASC clients, such as Housing, Planning and Benefits, so these may well need attention. For most DASSs the external partners in the health sector, i.e. GPs, Hospitals, and Clinical Commissioning Groups, will be a more important focus than other council departments. Effective partnership with these NHS players will make a very rapid impact on both ASC service delivery and budgets.

The third area, national influence, can be particularly satisfying (as well as offering a stepping stone to a national level job, should this be attractive).

Interestingly, when I asked Terry Dafter what he would like his legacy to be, he focused on:

- Firstly, innovation in how his organisation operates;
- Secondly, on policy values and their human impact; and
- Thirdly, on recognition of his role in shifting policy and practice nationally as regards Mental Health.

Both those last two are directly related to the experience of his own parents. In his own words:

> *"I want people to see that we were not afraid to change and innovate in the department. We did sometimes get things wrong, but actually we really believed in Personalisation. This new world that we are working in (including the new technologies) is fantastic. I think about my Mum and Dad and what they would get now compared to what they got back then.*
>
> *My dad had a stroke at 52 and was dead at 60. My mum was diabetic and had a stroke at 59 – dead at 61. She looked after my dad for many years because he was completely incapacitated by his stroke. Even though I was a social worker, I can remember how difficult it was getting some basic equipment for him. I rang Wiltshire Social Services where they lived only to be told 'oh no, you have to call another number' and being passed from pillar to post. Then it was 'you'll have to wait 4 weeks for it to be delivered, love – unless you'd like to collect it yourself'. So I had to drive to a windy industrial estate where a load of care equipment was just thrown down in a dirty warehouse and I was told*

> 'help yourself, mate'. It was just awful! And there was very little else on offer – a home help for a day or two perhaps.
>
> Now, we would issue a free prescription for the equipment that I could go and pick up from Boots or somewhere the next day. My mum and dad would probably have got small Individual Budgets. My dad never got out because he did not like the council day centre, but now he'd be able to spend that money on getting to his club for a drink occasionally. Mum was offered respite care but it could only be in a nursing home where everyone else was 20 years older than her. Now, she'd be able to use the funds for a day outing to Weston-Super-Mare where she grew up, which she'd have loved. That is a really good improvement in service.
>
> That's why I want Stockport to be known as open-minded and trying hard to make a good fist of Personalisation. This includes encouraging social enterprises such as Pure Innovations, which consists of former council staff supporting people with Learning Disabilities in gaining employment. It also encompasses good use of IT.
>
> I'm the national lead on Mental Health for the Association of Directors of Adult Social Services and I'm trying to get the country to move from 'Payment By Results' for mental hospitals because it incentivises them to keep people in psychiatric care with little opportunity for recovery. Instead, I'm trying to get us to move to 'Payment By Recovery', so that NHS Trusts are encouraged to work collaboratively with social care to move people on.
>
> I want to leave a bit of a better world than when I started and be remembered for making a modest contribution to the mental health system being less skewed towards acute care.

The best leaders are modest, as is well documented in the management handbook *Good to Great* (Jim Collins, Random House 2001) Often the influence wielded by a DASS both locally and nationally is done quietly and behind the scenes, a good example of which being Peter Hay's efforts to manage the collapse of the Southern Cross care homes company.

Why is social care not seen as attractive by ambitious people?

I've set out many satisfactions that can be gained from a leading role in ASC, but it is not generally regarded as an attractive career choice for people with any ambition. There are various reasons why that is the case. You can judge for yourself how good these are:

Financial

Let's compare the remuneration of a DASS with a Chief Executive or Director in a private company with a similar turnover and level of staffing.

Nottinghamshire County Council is on the large side, providing services for over one million people. Here's what their website has to say about David Pearson, their DASS:

David Pearson

As Director of the Adult Social Care, Health and Public Protection department, David is responsible for a budget of £301 million, providing health and social care services for 20,000 people every week.

A further 16,000 people each year receive housing-related support organised by the department.

> The department works with over 300 organisations who provide services to the value of £225 million. The care providers are drawn from the voluntary, statutory and independent sectors.
>
> David also has responsibility for the Council's Emergency Planning, Registration and Trading Standards Services.
>
> David deputises for the Chief Executive when he is away and also leads on initiatives across the Council. This has previously included leading on performance of the authority and service reviews.
>
> The department has been recognised for its excellent service programme to help older people live at home by the external inspectors.
>
> David has overseen the successful implementation of the introduction of personal budgets to all service users who receive adult social care services in community based services.
>
> A number of services have received national recognition during David's time as Director, including the national Audit Office's on the support available to adults with Asperger's Syndrome; reference in the 2012 Care and Support White Paper to schemes for disabled adults in employment and national recognition of the development of micro providers who are providing social care.
>
> David has been responsible over the last two years for leading the successful work on the transfer and integration of Public Health into the County Council. He has also led on the development of the Health and Wellbeing Board in the County Council with our partners. This has responsibility for the implementation of plans to improve the health and wellbeing of people in Nottinghamshire with our partners in Health and other public services.
>
> In 2012 David was voted one of the top 30 leaders in adult social care in the country through the Care Talk magazine.

Source: *www.nottinghamshire.gov.uk*

It's a responsible and demanding post. Senior managers are expected to be on call at all times, including weekends. Nottinghamshire County Council does not at this time provide any benefits that an equivalent senior manager in the private sector might receive in addition to the basic salary - such as performance-related bonuses, private health care or company cars.

His total salary for the financial year 2013–14 is £126,371 plus pension contributions of 18.3% (i.e. £23,126). His expenses are also quoted on the website and are very modest compared to anyone of similar seniority in the private sector.

Another example: a Deputy Director of Adult Social Services in the London Borough of Bexley in 2013 is paid under £82,000 p.a. (including allowances) plus a generous 20.6% pension contribution. Bexley's population in the 2011 census is 232,000 – about average for an English local authority with social services responsibility.

By comparison, a director in a moderately successful private company, holding responsibility for an operation of equivalent size, is likely to be earning between two to five times these amounts.

Within the social care space, Barchester Healthcare is a private company which looks after more than 10,000 people in over 220 care homes. In 2011 they had a turnover of £406 million and their highest-paid director earned £864,000, including accrued pension and lump sum payments. (Source: _worksmart.org.uk_).

Here's another example, this time from outside the sector: Laithwaite's, a wine home delivery company. In March 2013, they announced a turnover of £353 million. The two founder directors appointed their three sons as fellow directors in 2012. Between them they received £1.37 million in share dividends alone: that's an average of £274,000, not including any salary or pension contributions. (_The Guardian_, 20 March 2013)

Barrett Steel Limited is the biggest independent UK steel

stockholder. In 2012 turnover was £201 million and a loss of £6 million was reported. Nevertheless, the highest paid director earned £622,000, including accrued pension and lump sum payments. (Source: *worksmart.org.uk*).

Finally, here's another instance from within the social care sector: the charity Scope, campaigning and offering services for disabled people. In 2012, its three top managers all earned between £110,000 and £140,000, excluding employer pension contributions. Scope had a turnover of £101 million, considerably less than Nottinghamshire adult social care. (*Scope annual report for year ending 31 March 2012*)

In the past, working for the public sector had compensations in terms of more job security, good pension entitlement and a culture of better work-life balance (i.e. fewer working hours). Nowadays that is hardly true at all.

Furthermore, I would argue that the personal pressures and responsibilities in the public sector are actually greater than at an equivalent level in the private, given that there is a wider set of stakeholders to manage and more risk of unfavourable media coverage.

The 'Glamour Factor'

So many young people want to go into the media, or fashion, or music, or marketing, as these are considered glamorous professions. ASC could scarcely be less glamorous. If you are working for a council, then it will be primarily concerned with poorer people (because anyone with modest capital assets or income is means-tested out of eligibility for support.) By definition, the clients you deal with are ill or otherwise frail and in need of support. And yet it does not have the social cachet of, say, being a consultant in the health service.

It's also unlikely to offer much opportunity for international travel!

In a world that has become obsessed with brand recognition, local authority ASC tends to be very little interested in public branding. Even if the Council itself does invest in positive branding, this is rarely very successful. Charities are generally far more effective in this area – they have to be in order to keep the donations rolling in. Still, at least people may get a vague sense of you doing good if you say you are working in ASC.

So what is the role of the DASS?

'The buck stops with me' as Terry Dafter put it. In a legal sense, this is quite simply true, insofar as a local authority's responsibility for ASC is concerned.

Parallel to the development of child protection policies, there has over the last few years been an increasing emphasis on the importance of safeguarding adults. Vulnerable adults can be subject to various forms of abuse – physical, emotional, often financial – from those around them who ought to be caring for them, whether these be professional care workers, family members, friends or neighbours.

Another explicit duty that has recently risen up the priority agenda is to provide good advice and guidance to the whole population of your area, not just those (less than 4% of the population) who are eligible for council support.

Compared to many public sector jobs, a much greater proportion of the role is concerned with commissioning services from the private and not-for-profit sectors. It is now 30 years since in-house staff and care homes delivered most of local authority ASC provision.

The day-to-day responsibilities, however, are managerial: recruiting and developing staff, managing budgets and organisational processes and structures. And yes, it IS a matter of running a bureaucracy. So . . .

If that is your calling, **be proud to be a bureaucrat!**

Bureaucracy is universally a term of abuse these days, but let's just explore for a moment what it means.

OK, it literally means 'ruling from a desk' and it certainly is no longer acceptable (if it ever was) to sit in your large personal office, behind your kingsize desk, issuing edicts and receiving your underlings in order to give them instructions.

In the popular mind, bureaucracy is associated with endless 'form-filling' and 'box-ticking', and it can't be denied that social services have become very much identified with these soul-destroying activities. To make things worse, the public sector has been slower than the private in moving away from paper forms filled out by officials towards online self-service and telephone call centres. To be fair, this is partly because many of its 'customers' (especially in ASC) enjoy less access to those media, while the intimate and often complex nature of interactions with clients means that face-to-face meetings – usually in the client's home – are necessary for assessment and care planning.

Why do we need so much form-filling? Well, generally it's about gathering the information the council needs in order to approve the use of its resources on an individual's behalf. Those resources come from you and me, the tax-payers, and we have a right to know that they are being used appropriately. This needs to be documented so that it is seen to be fair and can be audited and checked where necessary. The public purse is dependent on the taxpayers' willingness to contribute, and resources need to be rationed in order to use them most effectively. There are essentially two forms of rationing:

- the competitive market, where whoever can spend the most money is able to purchase the scarce resource, or
- the 'bureaucratic' process of democratically agreeing the rules by which society agrees to share out certain resources so that the poorest and weakest do not suffer in the selfish scrimmage of the free market.

The key is to ensure that the necessary form-filling is appropriate, not too burdensome, easy to follow and keeps up-to-date with technical and other social developments.

That is why we need good bureaucrats who can show a degree of flexibility and adaptability and deliver the mandate that we collectively have given them over our socially-shared resources. This has been a particular challenge during the recent rollout of Personalisation: to reduce the level of council control while still retaining equitable and auditable processes. Fortunately, there is now a trend away from the need for every single little action to be auditable (something which has particularly bedevilled children's social care under the so-called Integrated Children's System). There is also a recognition that councils and their staff could take a few more risks and that citizens themselves might also be willing to share these risks. Some early adopter councils (e.g. Oldham) exploring Individual Budgets developed procedures for probing the risk factor in individual support plans. Were social workers and their clients, considering care options that were more risky than the traditional ones, more likely to meet the real emotional outcomes desired by the clients?

Devising and implementing these processes requires a regular new supply of good senior bureaucrats with the necessary brain power and people skills. It also requires leaders who are not afraid to take decisions that will be unpopular in some quarters and whose outcomes may not always be predictable.

Could you be one of those leaders?

Chapter Eight
Your local circle of care

If you're not attracted to the role of the DASS as leader in ASC, then you may be more suited to being 'just' a significant local influence in your immediate circle of care.

Actually, in this more localized role you can usually have a much more immediate and direct impact on people's lives than would a senior manager. You can create and lead your own circle of care. By this I mean that you can have a circle of people who look to you for a lead as regards care: these may be peers amongst your staff, carers or people themselves in need of support. You may not have any formal status or official recognition for playing this part and yet you will be having an influence and you will be appreciated – at least by some people.

Your influence may be subtle and pass unnoticed by those actually on the receiving end of it. In May 2011, I organised the UK visit by one of the world's foremost proponents of traditional African ways of healing, Dr Malidoma Somé. I took it as a great compliment when he remarked, with regard to my organisational skills in managing the dozens of people on his retreat, that I was effective in little ways that the participants would not even appreciate.

There are lots of ways you can manifest this role, e.g.:

* as a dedicated social worker, you can be a fount of inspiration for other social workers, by virtue of your enthusiasm, your experience, or your specific knowledge about a topic (LA processes, the law, IT systems, particular types of care or specific medical conditions, the best care providers, etc.)
* as a voluntary organiser of events for people in your community who need support, or for their carers. (Meg Barbour, referenced earlier, is a great example of this. Much to her embarrassment, she was honoured as Carer of the year by the local DASS whilst I was in process of writing this book.)
* as manager of a care home
* as co-ordinator of home care workers
* as an exceptional self-employed Personal Assistant (PA), accumulating satisfied customers ready to recommend your services to their friends and perhaps inspiring your own friends to become PAs
* as an adviser or support broker with a charity directly helping a circle of people and being a reference point for peers.

There are thousands of women and men up and down the country taking a leadership role in ways such as these, even though they would probably never consider themselves as 'Leaders'.

Here are three stories of people making a difference outside of local government, which featured in an article in The Guardian Social Care Network, 1 Oct 2013, written by Saba Salman (@Saba_Salman). They include tips on the qualities needed to be effective in your role.

This article may be found at:

http://www.theguardian.com/social-care-network/

Social care jobs in the voluntary sector

Three people with care and support roles for charities describe the challenges and rewards of jobs beyond local government

Nessa Killeen-Mcguirk is an integrated family support worker for Pact (the Prison Advice and Care Trust)

"My role, which I've had since 2008, bridges the gap between women in custody and their families. Sometimes families feel they've hit a brick wall in dealing with the prison authorities or in relations with their relative in prison – that's where we come in.

I meet prisoners at their induction, I contact their families – that could include grandparents or carers looking after the prisoner's children – and I make referrals to children's services if there are any issues we have like organising supervised contact visits. Some 200,000 children a year are affected by parental imprisonment. I liaise with the offender management or resettlement officers because it's known that prisoners are less likely to offend on release if their families are involved in resettlement plans.

I was a counsellor at the Rehabilitation for Addicted Prisoners Trust before this, and I wanted to broaden my experience of working with prisoners and families.

One challenging issue is the volume of clients – I have between 40 and 50 at one time. You have to be adaptable – I give ongoing support to some families for a long time, but others I support for only a few months.

You can't be judgmental and you have to communicate effectively and be sensitive to different perspectives; you have to be mindful of what the family and the prisoner tell you and listen in confidence while supporting both parties.

My work's interesting because each family's unique and has had a different experience. For some, prison is a familiar place but for others it's their first time.

One of our clients was estranged from her sister who was looking after her daughter. Neither the sister nor the prisoner's daughter were coming to visit, but we talked to both sides and encouraged them to reunite. Now the family is more supportive and comes to the prison's monthly family day.

We get such positive feedback from families and prisoners, mainly they feel they've been listened to and allowed to tell their story. Quite often, when I ask family members who's supporting them – because I'm supporting their relative who's in prison – they break down, because no one has asked that before.

It's rewarding to know that we listen to people and support them in what can be an unfamiliar and daunting situation."

Sue Greaves is older people's advocacy co-ordinator at Age UK Norfolk

"I've been with Age UK Norfolk for five years. Before this, I managed an advocacy service in Essex.

We provide a free, confidential service in residential homes, private homes, or hospital, helping people access information and working out how to resolve problems. Until recently, we had dedicated care home advocates in many local homes, but funding cuts mean we now have a floating service where our advocates for older people visit clients in various settings.

I oversee a team of 40 trained volunteer advocates (we have 125 volunteer advocates in total). People can self-refer or come via social services or a health professional, I do the initial assessment visit (to see how we can help) before sending out a suitable advocate.

Common issues involve benefits, financial issues or family disputes. Or someone has to sell their home and move into care, but they've no idea about residential care or how to sell the property.

Your local circle of care

Small things make a difference. A colleague worked with a very withdrawn client in a care home. He had a learning disability and was estranged from his family but his end of life plans had to be agreed, which is something families usually help with. The advocate discovered he had a passion for birds and installed a bird table at the home. The man not only began talking to other residents who shared his interest, but the advocate used the birds to talk about life cycles as a way into discussing and sorting out his end of life plans.

It can be challenging because, given our advocacy is issue-based, we stop seeing clients when their problem's resolved. But clients may regard that regular contact as a lifeline and they feel isolated otherwise.

You need patience and a sense of humour. You have to be assertive but not aggressive. Listening skills are important and you have to enable someone to make their own voice heard – not simply speak in their place. It's an enabling role; I like being able to fight someone's corner.

You might not always be able to resolve an issue – that's where managing expectations comes in – but it's very rewarding helping people change their lives.

The best thing a client can say is 'thanks, I don't need you any more'."

Robert Templeton is director of social work at SSAFA (the Soldiers' and Sailors' Families Association)

"We support anyone currently serving or who's served in the army, navy or RAF, with a range of social work services in the UK and overseas, we also support their families. Our services include family support groups (for example, for bereaved families), adoption services for serving families, support for families whose children have disabilities or additional needs and we run a confidential helpline.

My background's in local government and I used to work at SCIE (the Social Care Institute for Excellence). What attracted me to this job was getting back into hands-on social work and management. I oversee about 90 professional social work and family support staff.

Much of the work is similar to that in regular social work departments, but the difference is we're a hugely dispersed workforce. Our services stretch from bases in Scotland to Cornwall to overseas in the Falklands, Brunei or Germany. Part of my role is making sure we have consistent practice in those areas.

Military families often face different pressures compared to their civilian counterparts; many are away from home for the first time in a foreign country far from family and friends and some have to live as single-parent families while their partner is away on deployment.

One challenge is the physical distance between our staff and making sure we have consistency in a diverse set of contexts – each host country and its system is different. Another issue is working with bereaved families and ensuring we retain a neutral stance.

To be a social worker with us, you need to work fairly independently because you might find that your manager is thousands of miles away, not even in the same timezone. We always have a team manager available 24 hours a day, but you need to be motivated and independent. You also need to be able to listen, act on concerns and to think about different overseas contexts you're working in, some knowledge of how the military works can be an advantage too.

It's amazingly varied work; you could be helping a family struggling with looking after a child, or supporting bereaved relatives or supporting military families to resettle back in the UK.

The most rewarding element is meeting the people who use the service and seeing the positive impact of our support."

http://www.theguardian.com/social-care-network/

Your local circle of care

Sometimes your actions in these roles (and indeed anywhere in life where you show initiative and enthusiasm) may have far wider and longer-lasting effects than you yourself even realize. The little pebble thrown into the pond may vanish with a small splash, but its ripples will continue to spread ever wider.

You may be the butterfly flapping its wings that helps create a hurricane the other side of the world.

Just have faith that this type of local, quiet leadership will also pay off for you personally over time, perhaps in ways that you never expected. It may lead to new friendships or to life-long relationships. You will certainly gain respect from the people who do recognise what you contribute. It may lead directly to new job opportunities, or at least be something that you can reference in a CV. It may also lead to other sorts of opportunities, such as an article in the local newspaper, an interview on the local radio station, or a feature in the social care blog community. Give it a try as you embark on your first couple of years in ASC.

Chapter Nine

Making money out of delivering ASC

If you are lucky, you can:

- *Be a Capitalist!*
- Make a good living, *and*
- Help lots of people with care and support needs!

Actually, you have to be lucky *and* determined *and* pretty hard-working.

Why lucky?

Well, this chapter is primarily about running your own business in adult social care, and for that you need to have access to a certain amount of **CAPITAL**. Regrettably, this is not a resource that most of us are born with. So here already is one way in which you might be lucky: if you have wealthy parents, access to significant capital won't be such a problem; or you may be presented with the necessary start-up capital for your business idea by virtue of a beneficent legacy from an elderly relative.

If you don't come into some family cash, then you will need to find capital in other ways. It may not be easy: the nail-biting TV show 'Dragons' Den' gives some idea of the hoops you might have to jump through in order to successfully pitch your business idea to a prospective venture capitalist. Or you may be able to build up your own working capital, perhaps helped by a sudden windfall such as a redundancy payoff – this reward for years of service can, if you are lucky, be just enough to get you going with your own business.

How much is enough capital?

Of course, it depends on how you plan to earn your living. If you want to be an independent Personal Assistant, for example, then you will need money for the following:

- ✓ training (check out this example of a new scheme run by Oxfordshire County Council: *http://www.takingcontroloxon.org.uk/pa*)
- ✓ professional insurance
- ✓ some marketing materials (unless you already have an employer lined up), such as flyers, business cards, and a

website
- ✓ and, crucially, enough cash to tide you over between jobs (unless your personal outgoings are very low and you can survive on benefits if necessary).

'Enough' could mean just a few hundred pounds, or it could mount up into the thousands if you need to do lots of marketing and already have significant financial commitments.

An independent PA will normally, for tax purposes, be a sole trader and, unfortunately, is unlikely to earn sufficient to support a really comfortable family life.

Once you are considering running a company, your capital needs will expand considerably, as you encounter all sorts of necessary expenses:

- the cost of setting up your company
- insurance premiums
- book keeping and accountancy fees
- marketing, including a professional looking website
- essential IT equipment, at the very least a computer and smartphone.

Still, if your services consist only of yourself and your skills, or a simple product not requiring significant development, then you can make a start with a couple of thousand pounds.

In the 1980s, as councils moved away from delivering all their social care services with directly employed staff and out of their own capital resources, there was a growth in small, often family-run, businesses which filled this gap in care provision. There were two main types:

- home care agencies and
- care homes.

Home care agencies required very limited start-up capital. What they did need was a pool of staff willing and able to deliver personal care in people's homes. Initially, these were likely to be former council staff made redundant; later, increasingly, many would be immigrants prepared to work for the typically low wages. You would also need an office and, to give you some security, a 'block contract' with the council that guaranteed a certain amount of work over a given period. The office could be a converted garage or a rented space in the town centre, with just a desk and a phone for the staff co-ordinator and administrator.

Andrene's story

After some years as a care worker, Andrene Lewis-Longwe founded Break Barriers in 2009 and within four years was employing 16 staff with a projected turnover of £¼ million. This is her story.

"I grew up in Jamaica. In Jamaica, you look after your family. This morning, I heard the Minister, Jeremy Hunt, talking about how we should all look after the old people in our families more and I thought 'too right'. I came to England after the death of my last grandma, my father's mother. She had cancer. I nursed her until her dying day. I was 17.

My mother's mother was the same. I grew up with her. When her time came, all her children were abroad, so I was the only female in the household. She was at home with me caring until she passed. It was the month Princess Diana died. After that I decided to try for something new and come to England.

I had no idea what England was about. I started an NVQ Level 2 in Care. I had been a secretary in local government in Jamaica. I got a job with a Home Care Agency as a care worker.

The first assignment was for someone with a Physical Disability which I knew nothing about. I told the customer but the lady said 'just come'. I got there and thought 'Oh my G–, what have I let myself into?'

Caring came naturally to me. It felt like being at home. Things were just flowing for me.

I wanted to leave the assignment with the extra care home and take on other jobs through the agency, which paid more. The company running the home was like 'No, please work for us'. The lady I mainly worked for really liked what I brought to her care. So I took a permanent job and that is where Break Barriers started. I stayed there until I had had enough working for other people.

First, I studied for NVQ Level 3 while at the company and they made a Junior Manager job for me. I went on with NVQ Level 4 and completed the three year course in a year and a half, I was so self-driven.

I was Assistant Manager with the same Home Care agency for seven years. We had a unique service supporting 15 clients in a home and I was earning £24,000 at the end. The NVQ training was great in terms of developing a professional culture. It made it easy to spot things that were not going so well. The agency was very supportive.

I realised that customers wanted to go on outings and holidays. With the introduction of Personal Budgets, they got the chance to save up for trips by cutting back a little on other support. I decided to set up Break Barriers specially to help people with care needs get out of their community on recreational outings. We take people on holidays abroad. We offer care with transport and now we also offer more traditional home care (and that is the CQC category of our registration).

What motivates me is the sheer satisfaction of caring. I wish I could say that I had doubled my income but all the bills and staff have to be paid first. The joy I get is my customers'. I have just sent out customer reviews and am anxiously awaiting the returns. Nothing gives me more satisfaction. One social worker recently told me that she had never seen her client so happy since we took on her care.

The City Council are the most challenging part of the job. They do my head in. I only accept contracts direct from people with Personal Budgets or occasionally their own money.

I enjoy the leadership, setting a direction but I can be a silly-head sometimes. I am very lucky that my line manager from my previous company came to work with me as my staff manager a year and a half ago. She knocks the staff into shape and keeps them in line when I just want to have fun with them as one of the girls and boys.

My ambition is to continue to grow the business. My husband has joined me now with his commercial, driving and IT skills. He's started his Care NVQ Level 2. We've made Break Barriers into a limited company instead of a Community Interest Company because it is the future for us and our children and we need to be able to sell at some point.

I've been lucky so far. Beyond that, I might consider politics one day though I don't know which party. I've never voted but when I hear them talking about the problems of immigration I want to challenge them. I had to spend thousands to get residence rights here but I'm contributing and now providing employment.

What keeps me going is the sense of purpose and belonging. And finding the balance between professionalism and just being yourself with the customers."

Care homes and nursing homes, of course, require more substantial 'bricks and mortar' capital. Sometimes people might convert part of their own home into a care home. For example,

I met Amanda at a workshop at the Social Care Institute for Excellence (SCIE). She is what we now call a 'micro-provider'. Her son had a Learning Disability, so she and her husband had to learn all about looking after someone with LD. They decided to extend their property to make four bedrooms available for other people with LD. It was initially intended for respite care but, since there was insufficient demand, they became a residential home, retaining just one room for respite. This allowed them to be at home, available for their son, at the same time as making a living providing good care for others.

Shirley and Nelson's story

In the late 80s my good friend Shirley Askwith and her husband Nelson borrowed the capital to set up three care homes in Berkshire: Sandpipers, Nightingales and Kingfishers. Shirley was passionate about providing good care for frail elderly people. She was a trained nurse with a marvelous, loving way with people – clients, families and staff alike. This, combined with Nelson's business and accountancy acumen, provided a good living for them and their children in return for many years of very hard work and being on call at all hours. In the later years, their son also worked in the homes as a manager. Nelson and Shirley retired and sold the business in 2006.

Here are some things that Shirley had to say about it:

> "If you do things properly, you can make a living. If you don't, then you can make a fortune.
>
> It's the little personal touches that are so important – including physical touch if someone is upset.
>
> Kingfishers had 46 residents and every one would have their personal choice of daily newspaper with their breakfast (or Hello! Magazine in one or two cases). I was so saddened to learn that the new owners have restricted it to four newspapers for the entire home.

> *On Valentine's day, we bought a bunch of freesias for all the ladies and the gentlemen. The place smelled like a dream!*
>
> *Family visitors would be offered teas and coffees on arrival and, if they'd travelled more than 30 miles, a free lunch or dinner.*
>
> *I made sure that we paid staff top rates. Our Registered Managers were earning £35,000 back then.*
>
> *When interviewing staff, one of the first questions was always: 'Have you got the heart for this work?' Sometimes applicants would not quite understand and mutter: 'Oh, I'm not sure . . .' That would be the end of the interview and I'd tell them to come back another time when they did have the heart for the job."*

By the mid 1990s it was becoming increasingly difficult to run home care agencies and care homes profitably. Costs were increasing due to inflation and high interest rates. Moreover, the government and local councils were increasingly regulating providers to check that the services they delivered were of acceptable quality. This had become necessary following a few unfortunate examples of poor care and even abuse. Regulation imposes extra costs, both in terms of time spent on staff training, monitoring and form-filling and the capital expense of additional equipment and facilities. At the same time, local councils, who pay for approximately 50% of all home care and care homes, were trying to save money by driving down their operating costs. With profits declining, there was little money left over to repay banks or other investors, let alone to invest in improvements to the facilities and to pay the owners / managers. (Some providers, such as Barchester, decided not to rely on funding through local authorities but only to market to individuals who could afford their own care. This has proved to be a successful business strategy, as the councils have been squeezed over the last two decades while the wealthy have become wealthier.)

As is typical in a free market capitalist economy, there was a gradual process of business consolidation, with small family operations being bought out by the larger players. These larger businesses were often able to undercut the smaller firms by taking advantage of efficiencies of scale and by offering councils bigger contracts, sometimes at the expense of the caring ethos. Southern Cross care homes provides one example of this, where key decisions came to be made on purely short-term financial grounds, leading to its disastrous collapse in 2011. (This was only prevented from being even more disastrous for vulnerable residents thanks to some dedicated work by ADASS members, under President Peter Hay's leadership, together with some of the remaining Southern Cross managers.)

Why do I suggest you could be a Capitalist – and what does that mean?

Capitalism has had a bad name in many quarters since Karl Marx and Friedrich Engels published 'The Communist Manifesto' in 1848. After the fall of the Berlin Wall in 1989 and the collapse of state communism in Eastern Europe, it seemed as if capitalism was the only game left in town. However, in the absence of proper regulation, it didn't take long for its inherent weaknesses to manifest in the catastrophic financial crash of 2008. All of us in the western world are still reaping the consequences of this debacle.

When I say that you could be lucky and become a capitalist in adult social care, what I mean is that, by virtue of investing substantial capital resources in your business and directing the efforts of a sizeable workforce, you could be not just providing essential care and support to the needy public, but also generating a significant personal income. I am talking a starting point of perhaps a million pounds, which, at least in some parts of the country, is enough to own and operate a care home and certainly enough to set up an agency for care staff of various types.

At the risk of disappointing you, this is still a long way off from being a 'plutocrat' (from the ancient Greek, meaning a ruler based on wealth). Plutocrats are the proverbial 1% who really control most of the world's wealth and resources, as well as, in many countries, funding or otherwise directing the political system. To even be considered as a plutocrat your wealth has to run into billions of pounds.

Capital is just one of the crucial resource inputs in our society. It not only **pays for**, but also in a sense **consists of** all the buildings, equipment, roads and other infrastructure that we rely on. We give these assets a value in cash terms so that they can be compared one with another and traded. We expect any asset to deliver a value, and where the asset has to be created, then that value is known as the 'Return on Investment' (ROI). This may be expressed as a cash value, possibly interest that has to be repaid to a bank or other investor.

The other essential resource inputs are human labour and natural resources. Natural resources such as:

- arable fields for crops,
- sunlight and rain,
- minerals to be mined

All of these are dependent on the application of human labour to deliver value.

All the capital assets that we take for granted, the 'public goods' such as buildings, tools, roads, sewers, electricity and communication cables, have been created out of the labour of those who went before us (and to whom we should be grateful).

The problem, you see, is not with capital as such. Nor should we worry about the expectation, by those who own capital, of a due return on their investment, whether this be in a care home or any other business. (Let's just side-step the related question about the moral and social fairness of some people inheriting huge amounts of money, enabling them to settle back on their inherited capital and live the life of Riley.)

The problem lies in **Monopoly**. (Not the game, silly!)

There's a good reason why this game has remained popular: it provides a good education in how the capitalist system functions, and illustrates its fundamental, seductive danger. Under the free market capitalist system, company directors are legally obliged to maximize the profits for the shareholders who collectively own the company. That is their over-riding objective. Therefore they will always try to build their company into as much of a monopoly as possible. The more dominant a company is in a particular market, the more able it is to set the prices, in the absence of alternative suppliers. Ultimately, if you are a monopoly, you do not need to worry about the quality of your service because people will be forced to use it anyway. (This, by the way, was the problem in Eastern Europe under Communism, where an undemocratic state ran a total economic monopoly.) In the game Monopoly, this is simplistically but cleverly represented by the fact that if you own a set of matching streets you can then charge higher rents (and other players are more likely to land on your property).

In adult social care, one of the reasons why Southern Cross fell into disarray was that it grew large enough, no doubt spurred on by its greedy private equity investors, to monopolise the market in some areas. In the field of computer systems for social services departments, there was, for a time in the 1990s, a duopoly of suppliers: that is, there were two dominant suppliers who could to some extent act as a cartel to fix prices, even without explicit open collusion.

Any sort of monopoly position gives you power and, human nature being what it is, the owners of that power are likely, sooner or later, to start using it for their own benefit and to the disadvantage of others. Microsoft attracted widespread suspicion and resentment amongst certain people owing to its dominant, near monopoly position in the IT market, which it sometimes used to exclude other newer, smaller IT companies. To be fair, they did have great products which people liked to use and they were fast in exploiting and marketing their ideas. It made founder Bill Gates the wealthiest man in the world; he has since, to his great credit, used his unprecedented wealth in a positive way by creating the charitable Gates Foundation, which has done more than any other organisation (including the United Nations) to combat major diseases in Africa such as malaria and AIDS.

I am making this point to show that you do not need to be shy of taking the initiative in making money and building up capital. By all means bring your dedication and willpower to your chosen area of enterprise. The power you can build up as a successful business person can be harnessed to positive use, both benefitting people in need of care and support and providing satisfying employment.

The one thing that I learned in three years studying Politics, Philosophy and Economics at Oxford University is that power is not a zero-sum game. Before that I thought that if one person had more power it would inevitably be to the detriment of another. Well, it ain't necessarily so. There just has to be a balance of power. In the words of President Kennedy:

> *"The men who create power make an indispensable contribution to the Nation's greatness, but the men who question power make a contribution just as indispensable, especially when that questioning is disinterested, for they determine whether we use power or power uses us."*

Wise words, which I am sure the current US president Barack Obama would echo, although, in deference to current political correctness, he would most likely substitute 'people' for 'men'. Mind you, Obama would probably still use the word 'Nation' where I would prefer 'World' . . .

To conclude this chapter: do consider combining your caring vocation with managing a business. If you are not financially minded yourself, perhaps partner with someone who is, as Shirley did with Nelson in the example above. It is possible to combine a commercial business with doing good for the people you care for and support – just be sure to keep the right balance. Remember the example of Emma Harrison, Chairperson of A4E, quoted earlier. Her greed and the lack of ethical systems in the business led to the loss of her reputation and that of her company (though it has to be said that she has hung on to her millions).

Even if you do not yourself have access to capital or do not wish to take on that responsibility, there are now a fair number of large commercial organisations operating in the adult social care sector which can be useful places to gain managerial experience. Just be wary of directors becoming too greedy and monopolistic. **As long as they have to compete for customers, there will be a market discipline to provide value for money and deliver good services.** Sometimes that discipline of the bottom line can be more effective than any number of governmental Performance Indicators, policy guidelines or targets. (Though not always and, of course, financial quantifiers completely undervalue the needs of those who do not have funds in the first place to express their choices through a market mechanism. That is why the concept of Personal Budgets was introduced – but that is another story.)

Chapter Ten

Social enterprises & charities – a growing 'third way'

The redrawing of the boundaries between the state and private business has encouraged the emergence of Social Enterprises as a 'third way' poised between the two, capable of a flexible response to the changing needs of our age.

The term 'Social Entrepreneur' describes someone who seeks to achieve a positive social objective for a particular community of people while also making a living out of it as an independent individual not underwritten by the state.

A Social Enterprise subscribes to a legal definition when it becomes a 'Community Interest Company'. A CIC is constituted just like a private limited company, with three key differences:

- it cannot pay out profits in the form of dividends to shareholders;
- it cannot sell its assets (including the company itself) to the benefit of its owners;
- it has to have an explicit 'community interest' objective.

Its community interest statement sets out the group of people for whose benefit it must operate. This could be the residents of a particular area, e.g. Salford. Or it could be all those belonging to some other category: for example, people with dementia or suffering from ME. Its capital assets have to be used for these people. This also means that if the company is sold or any of its capital assets transferred, then the new owners are obliged to use them for the same purposes, a principle known as 'asset-locking'. In all other respects, they can operate like commercial companies (unlike charities, which frequently have to set up a separate limited company for trading purposes).

CICs were introduced as a company structure by the last Labour Government and have been encouraged under the Coalition. They are a means by which government (local authorities, health trusts or quangos) can enable good managers from within the public sector to move part of their organisation into a more commercial structure without the publicly owned capital assets (buildings, etc) being exploited purely for private gain.

(It is interesting to speculate as to whether the CIC approach would have made for a better transition in Russia following the collapse of Communism. Essentially, the Russian state conducted a firesale of its public assets. The beneficiaries became an oligarchy of ambitious and often unscrupulous operators, flaunting their immense wealth and indulging their every whim whilst the majority of the Russian population saw their own living standards plummet.)

CICs can also be set up from scratch, should you be able to demonstrate clearly the social objectives that you are pursuing and that your primary motive is not to generate capital wealth for yourself. If you succeed in delivering a good service to your target group, you will still be able to make a good living out of running a CIC. There is no legal limit to the salary that can be paid – you just won't get some of the tax benefits available to people who own regular companies and receive dividends.

There are numerous examples of LA & NHS staff successfully forming social enterprises, but it is not easy and the number of lasting successes is limited. One successful case is Pure Innovations (*http://www.pureinnovations.co.uk/*), which set up as a charity when staff transferred out of Stockport Council in 2005. They support people with a wide range of disabilities including learning disabilities to 'make the most of what they can do' including finding and keeping paid jobs. As they put it:

> We are a values led, creative organisation and our objectives are to promote independence, increase choice and provide appropriate support to people to enable them to make the most of their capacity and potential.

What are some of the possible pitfalls?

Firstly, it can be a major culture shock to be exposed to the blustery winds of competitive commerce, unprotected by the shelter and security of the public sector. This applies to managers and staff alike. The cultural infrastructure of the organisation will need to be reinvented.

Sirona Care and Health, spun out of Bath and North East Somerset council social services and the local NHS Primary Care Trust, provides a good example of a social enterprise setting about establishing its own distinctive culture. Deriving its name from Celtic mythology, Sirona runs care homes and delivers community services. Talking to Dan Glaister of the Guardian in 2011, their Chief Executive, Janet Rowse, explained:

> "We asked staff if they wanted something that looked like the NHS or the council, or something different. They said, if you're going to do it, let's go for it." . . . The 1,700 former council and NHS staff now wear purple lanyards. Workers also sport purple shirts with rainbow collars, a move designed to make them more approachable to dementia sufferers.

> "Sometimes emotionally you hit something unexpected . . . Maybe it's something to do with 90% of our staff being female, but they have coalesced behind it. When we had our launch events . . . I'd never seen so many purple people in my life."
>
> *(Article by Dan Glaister, Guardian Professional, 25 October 2011)*

The IT infrastructure also has to be re-created. This may at first seem liberating but comes with costs in terms of managerial input and expense. IT systems must not be built in isolation from the business processes. These days, the two are so closely intertwined that it does not make sense to develop one without the other. Hence the premium placed on a key skill combination: the ability to re-shape and enforce new business processes in tandem with an understanding of how technological developments can assist in improving efficiency. Getting the timing right is critical to knowing where to invest energy and cash.

Stephen Sloss's **Salvere** is an example of a company set up with a clear IT infrastructure strategy from the outset – carefully designed to underpin its business approach. Their website (*http://www.salvere.co.uk/*) is clearly intended as a haven of calm and reassurance for those anxious about losing control in a swamp of bureaucratic jargon:

> Take control of your life with support from our website and our independent living advisors. We'll show you how to plan well, find support and buy care sensibly. No faff, no fuss!

Stephen found time to talk to me over the phone. The fact that this interview happened when it did is testimony to key values that underpin Stephen's approach to life: both a keenness to help and a respect for the honouring of commitments. Although we missed the initial time that was scheduled for the telephone interview due to an important meeting over-running, Stephen made repeated attempts to call me back as soon as possible that same afternoon, until we were able to complete the session as he had promised – in between other crucial meetings.

Stephen Sloss

How would you inspire new entrants to the ASC sector?

"Social work is moving into an exciting new phase – it is more multifaceted than ever before. In Adults Services, over the next three to five years the public will increasingly want professional support to be offered directly rather than everything being supplied by the state.

Therefore there is a need for assessment, support planning and specialist advice that the public can access. This could be from not-for-profit organisations or from single social workers going independent and it will offer opportunities for new social enterprise solutions.

The public sector will continue to shape the broad commissioning picture, but individuals will be in control of their own finances, whether from private resources or from the state, and will be able to use it, for example, to support the services provided by private brokers. This is creating a new space. In the statutory sector, adult care will be increasingly focused on the complex situations around mental health, learning disabilities and older people.

Aren't the current cuts in social worker staff levels by LAs a threat to the profession?

Professionals need to become more entrepreneurial in response to the staff cuts by local authorities.

It is true that less will be spent on support per head and it

> will be delivered more quickly, but only 40% of people get any statutory assistance at the moment. The rest go without any support planning. This represents a market that will open up to people with social work training.
>
> In fact, there will be new apps, tools, advice and assistance for what we now call 'support planning'. In future it will be more about specifying what we want as individuals and sourcing it through DIY self-help.
>
> **Do you agree that SEs can bring increased flexibility and innovation?**
>
> A Social Enterprise is just a business but, since it is not-for-profit, it can operate in a way that is reassuring to customers. A CIC is asset-locked. That gives confidence to public sector customers as well as private clients. If you are spending your mother or father's hard-earned cash, you need to be able to trust the service provider.
>
> **Does it not make it harder to raise investment?**
>
> Yes, as a CIC it is harder to raise investment if a venture capitalist is looking for a return. A CIC is in it for the longer term and that becomes a marketing edge: 'we are a trusted supplier which is not going to be sold off'.
>
> It is early days for SEs. It will be interesting to see how they develop. SEs will have to compete on price and quality, since a good commercial business can do just as well as an SE."

If cash is short – which it invariably is – then being a social enterprise can only make things more difficult. It can be hard to raise investment capital for a social enterprise. Venture capitalists with cash to invest will naturally be keen to see a return on their investment; they are accustomed to their investment taking the form of share holdings, which they can then sell at a good profit if the company is successful and which may also pay out a dividend. That is not how CICs work.

On the positive side, SEs do provide more flexibility for staff and managers than these enjoy within local government structures.

This flexibility may arise from the way the service is shaped to better meet the needs of its vulnerable customers. It may also enable staff to adopt work patterns more suited to their personal circumstances, such as working from home or working irregular hours in order to fit with family commitments.

One of the effects of the internet age is that, whereas public sector bodies are often firmly restricted by geography, it has become much easier for small independent service or product providers to reach across geographical boundaries to locate their niche market.

Community Catalysts

Community Catalysts is an organisation that was set up to foster such small niche micro-providers, which need not necessarily conform to formal social enterprise structures. Here's what they say about themselves:

> Community Catalysts harness the talents of people and communities to provide imaginative solutions to complex social issues and care needs. We are a Community Interest Company established by and working in close partnership with the charity Shared Lives Plus.
>
> Headings like 'social care', 'health care', 'community' and 'housing' broadly describe the areas in which we operate but labels bring their own limitations. With this in mind we try hard not to limit our thinking to the conventional and are always willing and able to look for radically imaginative solutions that cross sectors and join up dots in unexpected ways.
>
> We work with local partners (local authorities, health trusts and other voluntary and private sector organisations) to stimulate and support the development of high quality and sustainable local enterprises.
>
> (_http://www.communitycatalysts.co.uk/_)

In recent years Social Enterprises have become increasingly fashionable, occupying a space between traditional, profit-oriented limited companies and charities. They often also share characteristics with worker co-operatives, where the company is owned by all the staff. Staff may have some say over directorial appointments and operations in general. All will benefit if the company is doing well, and conversely suffer if there are problems. John Lewis is frequently cited as a successful 'partnership' model for social enterprises – in their case running large department stores and Waitrose supermarkets.

Before I conclude this chapter, **charities** deserve a few paragraphs to themselves. There are some large and very influential charities operating in the ASC sector. Age UK is the first one that springs to mind: the merger of Age Concern and Help the Aged does in this instance seem to have created something greater than the sum of its parts. Others include Carers UK, The Alzheimer's Society, Scope, Leonard Cheshire, MIND, Turning Point, etc.

Many of these bodies reflect the whole gamut of public sector state activities, albeit on a smaller scale, focused on one topic or client group. They might comprise:

- a national policy unit that mirrors Whitehall and interacts with and influences government
- local advocacy groups that engage with the LAs & NHS locally
- a 'provider arm' that delivers services to the section of the public that they are serving
- fundraising activities, sometimes involving a separate trading body running charity shops, which give all their profits to the charity.

The larger charities therefore present characteristics of both councils and businesses, in terms of the processes and culture that they have to maintain. There are limited but potentially very satisfying career opportunities in the larger charities. Age

UK, for example, consists of 170 local groups across England. Many of these have turnovers running into the millions of pounds: Age UK's total income in 2011 was £156 million.

The Chief Executive's story

Paul Cann is Chief Executive of Oxfordshire Age UK, a local (and independent) branch of the national Age UK charity dedicated to improving the lives of older people. The organisation has a range of functions: providing advice, running services and managing their network of charity shops.

Brief personal background

"For me the drive to work with and for vulnerable people came from an awkward sense of the advantages of my upbringing. They were not 'Brideshead Revisited'-style advantages but just a stable family, with parents who were utterly devoted to ensuring their children had more opportunities than they had had. I was also lucky to attend a good state school, with two or three charismatic teachers offering inspiration. I ended up at Cambridge University not through intellectual brilliance or extraordinary personal diligence but through hard work, co-operating with, and climbing the frameworks of learning and progression placed caringly around me. This left me, in my early 20s, acutely aware of the dynamic tension between my own advantages and the horrendous disadvantages faced by so many.

Early career

I decided to start working life as a teacher because it was such an evidently valuable activity with such an immediate sense of one's effectiveness or not: you either get a spark or a clear sign of progress, or you don't. After trying different settings – teaching, Civil Service, private sector – I had a call from a head-hunter friend and took a position running a dyslexia charity. I immediately felt that I had landed in the right place, an environment of caring about people and about disadvantage. Crazy pay, unstable funding, a lack of conventional management culture, but deeply comfortable.

When did I realise I could really 'make a difference'?

I joined a charity, which had run out of money, but more importantly direction and self-confidence. The biggest thing I did was simply to pick up the flag that had fallen over and put myself alongside it, and with that act I committed my reputation and livelihood. I immediately saw that I could give heart to people toiling for their children and pupils.

My leadership role

I have had several Director positions, and five years ago I decided to switch from the national, policy-based perspective to the local, delivery-focused one. I run the older people's charity Age UK Oxfordshire, and we are above all about grassroots delivery . . . of everything from looking after people's feet to helping people and their carers cope with the final descent into dying.

I love the real-ness of this – no more 'holistic, person-centred health outcomes' and such jargon, but ordinary people struggling to cope being able to find more money or support. The most challenging part is the procurement roundabout: the public sector rulebook and procedure that ties us all up in knots for months when we could be getting on with connecting with disadvantaged older people.

My plans and ambitions for the future

The big difference I would like to make in future is to enable people to have a life, not just to survive: music, dance, words,

> *exercise, making friends, finding new partners. Often the policy agenda for vulnerable people is miserably poor in its ambitions.*
>
> **My advice to younger people considering a career in adult social care**
>
> *Believe that you could be doing the most profoundly valuable thing there is: connecting with people who struggle. It may not be fashionable, will not make you rich, but in terms of intellectual interest, scope for personal growth and leaving the world in a slightly different place ... unbeatable.*
>
> **With hindsight, is there anything I would do differently in my career?**
>
> *Build the craft of my career more steadily and not be so impatient.*
>
> **What personal values or beliefs or other supports have sustained me during the difficult times?**
>
> *I look to past leaders for the essential message about supporting the vulnerable. Most inspiringly, people like Jesse Jackson and his amazing election 'Keep hope alive' speech about and to the dispossessed of America in 1984. But the real anchor has always been my wife and our children, and the determination to see them OK.*

On the advocacy side, there is much heart satisfaction to be gained from representing your chosen 'client' groups – and, of course, empowering them directly as much as possible. At the level of national policy, this needs to be yoked to the intellectual challenge of carrying out or commissioning research and presenting the results persuasively to government. Responsibility for implementation, however, will not fall on your shoulders.

At the operational service delivery end, on the other hand, there will be needy people directly dependent on some of the services you offer. You may have to develop very effective business skills, whilst never forgetting the culture and underlying objectives of the charity. This can prove a difficult balancing act, even though, typically, such a position is less well rewarded financially than an equivalent post in a successful private company, or even in the public sector.

In a charity, much of your work is likely to involve organising volunteers and recipients of care and support. I will explore these roles further in the next chapter.

Chapter Eleven
Big Society and voluntary work

There has been something of a buzz around the concept of the 'Big Society' ever since David Cameron made it the lynchpin of the 2010 Conservative general election manifesto.

Since coming into government, the Conservatives, with Lib Dem support, have endeavoured to put its ideas into effect. Hence, we have the Big Society Network and the Social Enterprise Banks, because social enterprises are very much part of the Big Society vision.

It is easy to be sceptical of the phrase and see it as political cover for cutting public services to the detriment of the poor and vulnerable in society. It was clearly a key part of Cameron's strategy to 'de-toxify' the Conservative brand from the legacy of Mrs Thatcher, who had become identified with her notorious declaration: 'There is no such thing as society'.

Nevertheless, the Big Society concept is **not** primarily about volunteers replacing paid public sector staff. In fact, the principles behind Big Society chime perfectly with the values behind the Personalisation agenda within Adult Social Care over the last five years. Why? Because it is about empowering people and communities.

In fact, it could be argued that the Big Society concept is more in line with good social work thinking than the rather consumerist idea of Personal Budgets (PBs). The large and very worthwhile charity Turning Point works with many of the most disadvantaged and troubled people in society: alcoholics and drug users, the homeless, people with mental health problems. They have a strong track record in helping individuals turn their lives around. Their response to Personal Budgets was to promote what they called 'Connected Care', whereby the resources freed up for service users under PBs would be pooled within a local community organisation to build social capital and leverage the aggregate purchasing power of people's PBs. This is a much more 'socialist' approach (in the sense used in David Brook's excellent book 'The Social Animal') than the individualized consumer power ethos that underpins Personal Budgets as introduced under the Labour Government. (Though I do appreciate that they could be used as a lever to generate positive, disruptive change in the system. There was also an attempt to encourage self-organisation through 'ULOs' – User-Led Organisations.) *'The Social Animal: A Story of How Success Happens'* by David Brooks (2012) is a very readable account of recent findings in sociology and neurology – all wrapped up in a fictional story about two people's lives.

This is how Turning Point's Director for Connected Care, Richard Kramer, described their approach:

> *"Through Connected Care we've established a new way of working with communities. We ensure local authorities can engage with you, their residents. We listen to your needs and use your views to build better partnerships between statutory and voluntary sector agencies.*
>
> *There are three core elements to our approach:*
>
> * *Community engagement and capacity building*
> * *Integration and service redesign*
> * *Cost benefits.*

> *We recruit and train local people to work as Community Researchers. This gives you the opportunity to be pro-active in improving the quality of life for yourselves, your friends and family – within the local area."*

They reckon that for every pound invested with them, four pounds of public money is saved.

Richard Kramer's story

Richard originally qualified as a solicitor, has worked for a public affairs consultancy, NCVO, and was Mencap's Head of Campaigns for four years.

He has now moved on from Turning Point to become Deputy CEO at 'Sense', the charity for deafblind people. Here is his story and his take on the effects of current government policy – revealing, as of late 2013, a severe disillusionment with the so-called 'Big Society' aspirations of the Coalition Government.

> *"I have always been involved in disability. I grew up with learning disability in my family. I have worked in the field of learning disability in multiple roles: as a volunteer, as trustee of Respond, employed with Mencap and with Turning Point and more recently joining the deafblind charity Sense as their deputy CEO. Sense reaches out to deafblind people; supports them and gives them a voice. That is why Sense and I are a perfect fit – the organisation's values reflect my own.*
>
> *It was as a volunteer in a youth club for people with disabilities that I saw first-hand how timely support could transform disabled people's lives. In particular, art and*

music can really help people to express themselves. Twenty five years later disabled people are facing a triple whammy through cuts to personal income, cuts to disability income and cuts to social care. The concept of 'Helping those who need it most' has been lost. In other words, the cuts are not fair but targeted, and they target people in poverty, disabled people and their families. I strongly believe that we need to discover the better angels of our nature which feed compassion, which enable us to walk in another's shoes, which promote solidarity and which see the best not the worst in people.

I have worked in Mencap and Turning Point – both assertive organisations. I don't think we should be afraid if we feel strongly about something and have sufficient understanding of the subject to speak out. It is important to speak up for the most disadvantaged deafblind people who are affected by government policy. Our work makes us an authoritative and credible voice and we should use this voice to speak out fearlessly when needed but reflect the type of organisation we are– values based, evidence based, problem solving and solutions focused. Above all, people who are involved in formulating new policy need to have an adequate understanding of just how precarious the situation for people on low income has become.

At this time of great financial austerity, all public spending is under scrutiny. Every service funded through Sense needs to be able to demonstrate the difference it makes, including its long-term social value. As deputy CEO I am committed to assessing and articulating the value that our services produce, both for disabled people who use them and for society as a whole. That is what sustains me in my work."

One of the newer generation of Conservative thinkers behind the ideas of Big Society is Phillip Blond. Reading his book 'Red Tory' (Faber & Faber 2010) one is struck by his championing of working class organisation and history. One of the attractive characteristics of his thinking is his positive view of human nature: the firm belief that groups of people will band together to improve their lives collectively if they are given half a chance. It was the same belief in humanity's ability to overcome selfish consumerism that attracted me to Marxism when I was a young man.

As mentioned back in chapter two, my first job after finishing university, back in the 1980s, involved community self-organisation. It was a time of very high unemployment (even higher than now amongst young people). I too was unemployed and, together with with others in my community, set up a drop-in welfare rights and advocacy group for the unemployed and other claimants. We succeeded in getting a small grant from the local council that paid for an office, some basic office equipment and a part-time co-ordinator of the volunteers. It was for me an excellent experience in community organising and I will never forget some of the characters I met and the stories they told me – including their experiences in prison.

If you are not finding the employment you want or are simply not yet sure of what direction to take, then this is an avenue that you can explore. There will certainly be opportunities for you to get involved in local groups and take on a leading role, or even to set one up yourself with friends or acquaintances. Meg Barbour, quoted earlier, is an excellent example of someone who did just that, providing, with her luncheon club and group outings, an important social service for 30–50 people with dementia and their carers.

While Big Society is **not** just about organising volunteers, it does promote that approach and indeed we should not, in our 'age of austerity', undervalue such contributions.

Chapter Twelve

Policy is worthwhile — Never mind the gap!

In the last chapter I talked about 'Big Society', which is not so much a policy as one over-arching ideological strand for the current Coalition Government. It can be translated into policies in particular areas (and Jesse Norman offers some instances unrelated to social care in his book 'Big Society').

Personalisation and Personal Budgets are policies within ASC which I have already touched upon a few times. I don't intend in this chapter to argue the whys and wherefores or pros and cons of particular policies, but I would like to discuss them in relation to why, as you develop your ASC career, you might want to take on a role in shaping policy.

It's easy for people to become cynical about policy. There is a fair degree of cynicism about Personalisation in ASC at the moment, especially amongst traditional social workers. One thing about policy – just as with much advertising – is that the reality actually delivered frequently does not live up to the hype with which the policy was introduced.

Does that mean that policy development is a waste of time?

No.

Policy change can be valuable. Even if there is a gap between the intention and the eventual reality on the ground – never mind.

Policy is worthwhile – Never mind the gap!

All systems need fundamental change from time to time. In the last three decades we have experienced massive changes in technology, demographics and what people expect from life. ASC needs to be responsive to this. Any large system and organisation tends to become sclerotic and set in its ways over time. We see this in companies: Microsoft, for example, was incredibly innovative, pioneering and responsive in its early days but has become rather stale since its emergence as a capitalist behemoth in the late 90s. It's quite likely that Apple and Google are starting to go down the same road.

The same occurs in public sector organisations. It is natural for people to like the familiarity of a certain way of doing things. It becomes comfortable, especially for groups of professionals, to adhere to their particular ethos and practices, but sometimes these need to be challenged and adapted to suit changing circumstances. I am not saying that ***all*** change is good – certainly, we have had far too much organisational change in the NHS over the last 20 years, often focused on internal concerns rather than the real priorities of its users. It is well known that the last resort of a senior manager who wants to make an impression is to carry out an organisational restructure. The government politicians who run the NHS will always be always tempted to shake things up, simply in order to distinguish themselves from their predecessors.

In the public sector ***policy*** is the means by which established ways of doing things are challenged – hopefully for the better. It is about setting out a vision that can inspire and motivate people. In that sense, promoting a policy is an exercise in salesmanship, and your target market is a wildly disparate collection of staff, citizens, professional colleagues, academics, the media, and pressure groups, each with their own criteria of judgement.

You have to start by outlining the bigger picture. Some of the finer points may change as you start colouring in the details. Indeed you may not know what the details will really look like until you get there (though be careful not to admit this too

often!). If the policy is right, this won't matter.

Here is an exercise for you:

Exercise: Policy & Planning

Think of a plan or a project that you might want to put into practice. Try something nice like organising your next birthday party or planning a holiday. If possible, choose something that you are really going to do over the next months.

✻ **My Project:**

Now write down some phrases about it that get you excited; things that you are looking forward to when you achieve your project:

✻ **What excites me about my project:**

Policy is worthwhile – Never mind the gap!

You will have to persuade people to take part in it, even though it might cost them time or money.

Write down some phrases that you would use to persuade them why your project will be a good thing:

✳ **You should support this project because:**

and:

and:

OK, so they've said they might be prepared to support your project, but they'd like to know a bit more about it.

Think it through in some detail. Write down a long list of characteristics: things you are going to do; activities involved in the project; benefits for its participants; how they will feel afterwards. Include adjectives, descriptions, colours, emotions. Just words, phrases, short sentences – not long sentences or paragraphs. Get to at least 20 items – don't hold back – let it flow – you have to persuade these folks!

✳ **My list of what's involved in my project and what it will deliver:**

Policy exercise conclusion:

Right. Phew! That should have done it. They will really be up for it now!

Now, imagine yourself near the end of the project.

No doubt a few things have come up in your life during the weeks or months that it has lasted: perhaps some unexpected expenses or demands from people that you had not anticipated.

Have a look back at all the activities and benefits that you had listed.

Do you really think you will have delivered them all by the end of the project?

You may have found, in discussing your project's various aspects with your friends or colleagues, that one item or another was not actually a priority for them. They might have suggested replacing it with something a bit different.

Now look back at the reasons you gave for them to support the project.

Do you think you will broadly have met these?

Be realistic about how the project was likely to pan out in reality, and give yourself a score out of 10.

   ✳ **My score:**

Don't peek ahead.

OK, have you written it down?

If you have given yourself less than 10 out of 10, does that make the whole project worthwhile? Will you and your colleagues gain satisfaction and be better off than if it had not happened?

I would say so – as long as you are scoring higher than, say, a 5 out of 10.

Would you have got your colleagues on board if you had not sold them the benefits upfront? Probably not.

Would you have had the energy to complete the project if you had not been excited about it in the first place? No.

✶ **If this was an actual project for you, then try to recall how you felt as you were approaching completion. How close was the actual manifestation to your original fantasy?**

This exercise will have given you some idea of what writing policy is like.

Writing policy is, essentially, an attempt to visualize, in as much depth as possible, the ramifications of proposed changes. It is (generally) worth the effort involved – even if there is a gap between what it initially promises and the actual outcomes some years later.

Before an academic jumps up and down, I do need to qualify this and explain why I added the word 'generally' in brackets in the last sentence. Some policy is simply bad policy. Policy can be 'bad' for three reasons:

a) **Insufficient factual research** has taken place to ascertain the pros and cons and likely consequences of changes to be introduced. It is often stated that policy should be 'evidence-based'. This is a very worthy ambition, and the more evidence one can gather to justify a new policy the better.

However, the fact of the matter is that policy is intended to bring about a change – a new set of operating procedures – and in the complex social world we inhabit this can have unintended consequences: entirely accurate prediction is impossible, however much research is carried out. The important thing here is to monitor the effects and be prepared to modify the policy if there is clear evidence that it is not working – and avoid becoming fixated on ideology.

b) **Insufficient soundings** have been taken amongst those who will be affected by it. There will always be people who are opposed to a new policy which disrupts the way they are used to operating. There may be some individuals or groups who are genuinely disadvantaged by it, finding themselves worse off as a result. This is what utilitarianism (seeking the greatest good for the great5est number) and ultimately democratic politics is about (always provided that basic rights are maintained). If this has not been properly assessed in advance, then there is every possibility that a new policy will gather so much vocal opposition that you will be forced to abandon it – even if it would genuinely have improved overall happiness. It may simply have been a matter of poor salesmanship, or a failure to cultivate support from the beneficiaries sufficiently early. You'll know how introducing small changes within a family or group of friends can raise a complex pattern of ripples; imagine the potential for storm and stress unleashed by policy changes affecting thousands or even millions, on a local or a national scale.

c) The policy is being **promoted by a narrow pressure group** for their own benefit at the expense of the greater long-term good. In our increasingly unequal societies lobbyists are frequently paid to push policies for their wealthy clients, subverting the proper democratic process. (This has become particularly true at the level of the European Union where the media and the public generally pay less attention

Policy is worthwhile – Never mind the gap!

than at national government level.)

So, how can you get involved in policy making?

i) Local lobby group: concerned about a particular issue, say, such as the closure of a day centre.

ii) As an LA manager in ASC: e.g. deciding on the questions to be used in a Needs Assessment or Resource Allocation System; deciding whether to introduce a Call Centre approach as the first single point of contact for ASC Referrals.

iii) As a local authority councillor – particularly if you become a cabinet member for ASC: e.g. deciding on the charging policy for home care and day centres (under so-called 'Fairer Charging' rules); deciding whether to 'externalise' certain services or facilities; determining funding priorities between, for example, providing advice and guidance for all citizens, including self-funders, investment in more preventative services, or improving the quality and funding level for those in most severe immediate need.

iv) As policy researcher and then director within a national charity, political party or think tank like the King's Fund or Demos.

v) As an academic advising government on policy issues and researching the evidence.

vi) Within the policy team at the Department of Health or other Whitehall departments impacting on the adult social care world, e.g. Dept of Work & Pensions or Communities & Local Government.

vii) Ultimately as a minister in government!

Finally, let's take the example of **Personalisation**.

It will show some of the aspects discussed above.

Originally, this was encapsulated in the policy of introducing 'Individual Budgets' for adult social care recipients in England. Individual Budgets would be a single cash amount that a social care service user could receive (through the local authority) to support themselves. It was recognised that most service users were in receipt of a range of six benefits and services from different governmental organisations, including social services, Supporting People, Disabled Facilities Grant, health funding, return to work grants, etc. The policy was that all these different funding streams, administered by varying bodies with incompatible rules, would be combined into one in order to make things simpler for the citizen and to empower them to use the cash as they best saw fit rather than just accepting whatever service or equipment was provided by the state.

I clearly remember a small conference back in February 2007 where the then relatively new Director General for Social Care, David Behan, was propounding this policy objective. I had a background in benefits and financial assessment and asked the question whether this meant that primary legislation was going to be passed through Parliament in order to bring all the different means tests together. I was assured that 'yes, that would be done'.

It was a strong and compelling vision, delivered by David Behan with great passion. It was the beginning of what became known as the Personalisation policy. In the event, there was no primary legislation and the six different funding streams and means tests and administering bodies have not been combined. That does not mean that the IB policy was a complete failure. Instead it focused on the one area that was by far the largest in terms of funding and which was most directly under David Behan's control: adult social services funding and service provision. Individual Budgets aiming to combine the six streams became 'Personal Budgets' just for ASC funds.

Before I move forward in the Personalisation story, it is worth first going backwards in time to before David Behan's announcements on IB policy at the Department of Health. The fact of the matter is that the whole policy did not originate within Whitehall. As is so often the case, the ideas for the policy were developed by what we might call 'civil society' or particular pressure groups. In the case of Personalisation, this was specifically an organisation called 'In Control'. It emerged in the early 2000s, as people with Learning Disabilities and their carers became increasingly frustrated with the limited options being offered to them by way of LA support. People with LD were passive recipients of what the state offered instead of becoming empowered to live fuller and more satisfying lives. In Control developed a whole philosophy around active citizenship to justify what became the new policy of giving service users direct say over how, and with whom, the money allocated for their care was spent.

The approach was quickly picked up by other pressure groups, especially those of people with Physical Disabilities, and it was adopted across the LA ASC sector.

Here we need to mention the danger of unintended consequences.

There was one 'client group', the frail elderly, who did not initially benefit from Personal Budgets. This was pointed out by the very first research into IBs, the so-called IBSEN report, and indeed it remains unclear as to whether this group does derive any benefit. (The issue here is that frail elderly people are much less willing and able to take on the responsibilities associated with managing a direct payment of cash, which might include having to employ staff, with all the attendant complications. Over the years systems have been put in place to mitigate this problem – again, monitoring and adjusting initial policy in the light of experience.)

Unintended consequences can often arise from people 'playing the system': it may be the result of managers focusing only on those targets that the government is measuring, to the detriment of other areas, or it could be the product of an unscrupulous minority of the recipients 'gaming' the new policy to gain unfair advantages.

Nevertheless, there is a wealth of anecdotal evidence that, on the whole, Personalisation and Personal Budgets have brought real improvements to many people's lives. A couple of stories have already been mentioned in the chapter on clients & carers. Here is the story of a career civil servant:

Charlotte Buckley's story

Charlotte Buckley is the Deputy Director of People, Communities and Local Government, at the Department of Health in Whitehall.

Apart from the DH, she has worked for a number of central government departments including the Cabinet Office (as part of the Efficiency and Reform Group) and the Department for Business Innovation and Skills. Before joining the Civil Service, Charlotte worked as a management consultant and social researcher.

She worked on the 2012 Care and Support White Paper, as the lead on social care markets and provider failure, and on the Dilnot Commission.

My personal background

"I grew up in a small town, Heywood close to Manchester, and attended Manchester High School for Girls before obtaining a place at Corpus Christi College, Oxford University,

to read history, in 1998. Many members of my family have worked in public service, or made a strong social / public contribution, e.g. through charitable work.

My early career

When I originally started work, I was looking to move into a career in management consultancy – attracted by the intellectual challenge of this work and the variety provided by its project-based nature. My first role was in business intelligence looking at the financial services technology market. Whilst this work was interesting, I found it difficult to 'connect' to the subject matter. I therefore made a move into market and social research, working for a boutique market research agency completing quantitative and qualitative primary research – primarily in the education sector, with some public sector work. From here I moved on to work as a management consultant within a large national accountancy firm, specialising in public sector work.

It was during this role that I discovered a real interest in the public sector and decided to apply for the civil service fast stream. This offered a wide range of opportunities, significant mental / intellectual challenge on big, important questions that mattered and the chance to progress quickly. The complexity of public policy making was also highly attractive.

I really was very attracted to the chance to do something that made a difference – to everyone, rather than to an individual company – even though at this stage I was not quite sure what that 'something' would be.

On the fast stream I undertook a variety of different roles – regional policy, science and research policy, further education policy – and I completed a role as a private secretary.

Overall – I would say that my early career was characterised by trying to identify:

a) the type of work I enjoyed e.g. research and analysis,

b) what I found intellectually stimulating, and

c) areas of work that I felt 'connected to'.

When did I realise I could really 'make a difference'?

During my early fast stream career, I discovered a real interest in health and care policy. This intellectual challenge was coupled with my mum passing away from a degenerative disease – where I had first hand experience of health and care services and professionals. This led to me applying for a role in the Department of Health working on the 2012 White Paper – Caring for our Future.

In this role I found that improving the outcomes of those using health and care services was very important to me; and I felt that I could use my analytical, policy and negotiating skills to 'make a difference'. Although I may not have been helping individuals, I felt that I could use my skills at a national level to develop and encourage a better system, which should ultimately lead to individuals having better outcomes. This was strengthened by my time on the Dilnot Commission – looking at the new funding model for social care.

In terms of risks and worries, these were mainly focused around the complexity of the system and whether the good intentions sitting behind national policy initiatives would be delivered within a highly devolved system. I also felt it was important to not be captured by the 'Whitehall bubble' and lose sight of what mattered to real people.

My leadership role

I would characterise my leadership role as one of connecting the Department of Health to its key partners – including the NHS, Public Health England, local government, the voluntary and community sector – and the public. I see it as my role to translate policies and initiatives led from the Depart-

ment into something which is meaningful to those outside of Whitehall; and equally to take the real life issues – the challenges and opportunities – back into the Department.

The most rewarding aspects are:

a) Seeing how we are helping, usually through quite small steps, those who are working hard to support people, for example a voluntary project that we have supported through a grant.

b) Seeing the overall transformation that is taking place in social care, despite the challenges faced such as the financial context – with the focus on empowering people to have choice and control, the efforts to improve quality, and putting the system on a more sustainable financial footing. And feeling that I have played an important role in making that happen.

c) When someone recognizes that you are doing your best, even if the perfect solution is not possible.

Plans / ambitions for the future to make a greater difference?

I guess this is just to keep doing what I'm doing, only better.

What advice would I give younger people considering a career in adult social care?

I'm not sure that I can really answer this question adequately. In terms of advice in becoming a career civil servant, I think this would be to persevere – it is difficult to get a role in the civil service, but it is well worthwhile. Don't worry if you don't get the ideal role first time around – there are lots of opportunities to move around and to move up.

With hindsight, is there anything I would do differently in my career?

Not really. It may have taken me some time to work out quite what I wanted but this has all been invaluable experience. I also think I got to my 'leadership' role at the right time – and I wouldn't have wanted to get here sooner. By experiencing a range of different roles and types of work, I feel that I am more rounded and overall better placed to tackle the challenges that I face day to day.

Looking to the future, I would like to do more work directly with service users and professionals – I think this will make me a better leader.

What personal values or beliefs or other supports have sustained me during the difficult times?

Some mix of the following:

- *Work ethic – public service ethos. We are in a very privileged position in being responsible for spending public money and it is important that we make the best possible use of every pound.*

- *Perspective / balance – remembering that there are always moral, ethical, economic and social considerations to be weighed up.*

- *Individual stories – connecting regularly – going out to speak to people using services and those delivering them; to 'keep it real' and not let the intellectual exercise of solving the problem become more important than making it better for the most people that we can.*

- *Perseverance – sometimes you can feel like all the hard work has gone to waste (e.g. when there is a change in government or funding is reduced) but you need to continue to keep doing the best you can with what you have ..."*

There are those for whom policy making, instilling a clear sense of direction into what might well be a lumbering and unfocused operation, becomes a lifetime's passion, combining intellectual thrill with the satisfaction that comes from being one of life's movers and shakers.

"I'm a policy person at heart because if you change policy, you change it for everyone"

Martin Green's story

Martin Green is Chief Executive of the English Community Care Association. ECCA represents small, medium and large private and not-for-profit care providers. Martin was awarded an OBE for Services to Social Care in 2012. He is also Visiting Professor of Social Care at Buckinghamshire New University. This is his story:

> "I'm a Northumbrian and my family had no engagement with social care whatsoever. I did have an incredible teacher at school who engaged us in constant debate on current issues. I took sociology, history and religious studies at A-level and went on to do a degree in Sociology.
>
> My first job was as an Information and Development Officer for Gingerbread in the north of England. I had little clue, like most people in their first job, but great support from colleagues.
>
> [Author's note: Gingerbread is a charity that supports and campaigns for single parents. My mother was a member around the same time, in the mid to late 1970s, when single parenthood was still quite rare and many were rather ashamed of it.]

Then I moved to a council's Housing Department and was involved in implementing Housing Benefit in the early 1980s. It was my first engagement with bureaucracy, which brought home its difficulties but also the importance of having good systems.

After that I became Housing Policy Adviser for Age Concern Greenwich. A vacancy soon arose for the Chief Executive role in the organisation and there were two competing factions. I was the compromise candidate so at the age of 25 I was appointed Chief Executive, responsible for 30 staff. I just happened to be in the right place at the right time.

I was surrounded by an incredible team of supportive people. My PA, Jackie Grant, was spectacular. I promoted her to 'Director of Special Projects' and told her she'd be very busy doing all the things I couldn't do myself! She had great knowledge of the issues and deep understanding of what we were trying to achieve. She later became Chief Executive and was fantastic.

It was at Age Concern Greenwich that I discovered I could really make a difference. Our 30 staff were all policy people and we started to wonder if we should move into service delivery. I was persuaded that you've just got to try it and see if it works. Then we started getting feedback about how much difference we were making. Later, under Jackie, Age Concern became the major service provider for older people in Greenwich.

That's the thing in adult social care: there's a direct link between the decisions you make and people's lives. It is a powerful position but frightening. You have to have a clear framework for why you are making decisions. For example, making cuts in services can have huge impacts. You have to identify who you are working with and who you are not helping and where the greatest need is. So, when I discovered that 30% of people attending a Day Centre were driving themselves there, I decided to close it and shift the resources to supporting the people who were stuck in isolation at home.

I'm a policy person at heart because if you change policy, you change it for everyone. If you do casework, you are only helping those you work with. Before my current role, I was Chief Executive of Counsel and Care, a charity for the elderly. We carried out complex casework which then informed our policy work. We were able to ground policy development in the bad practice that we saw.

After Greenwich, I was Chief Executive of a brain injury charity for a while, but I got bored as it was really just about allocating money in research grants and funding intellectual debate. I left and worked for Unicef in Uganda on an AIDS / HIV programme. It taught me how to manage in the midst of chaos. There were no functioning telephones, an irregular electricity supply and huge civil unrest at the time. Also it took me five months to realise that, despite the same English language, the culture was totally different. I learned never to take things at face value but to enquire into the unseen stuff that is a motivator rather than what appears on the surface.

I then came back to England to become Chief Executive of Age Concern in Wandsworth. My predecessor was one of the best managers in the world and I had an amazing senior management team. I like an intellectual challenge, so became really bored and moved to be Chief Executive of Age Concern Lambeth which was the complete opposite: a dysfunctional organisation in the midst of a dysfunctional borough!

Six months later Lambeth Council appointed Heather Rabbatts as Chief Executive.

[Author's note: Heather, famously, was a black single mother and at the time the highest paid Chief Executive in local government. I met her myself while on a project for Lambeth and found her very incisive and to the point. Rather surprisingly, she later went on to become Executive Chairwoman of Millwall FC and the first woman director of the Football Association.]

Heather was an inspiring leader and there were many dynamic people at Lambeth, as well as a huge amount of dross. Heather's vision was always to put Lambeth residents first and remind the council bureaucracy that they were there to serve the residents and that the council's existence was not an end in itself. This mirrored my task at Age Concern.

We both railed against 'box ticking', which had become an obsession in the mid 1990s. People were appointed because they made the [ethnic] monitoring figures look good even though they were not the best for the job. And then they were given no support or opportunity to develop! The voluntary sector as well as the council had to change. With Molly Evans, a fantastic black community leader, we founded Lambeth Voluntary Action Council. It caused some divisions and I learned how to manage conflict and the importance of finding allies – the people who have the same vision as you. In that situation you make some really long-lasting personal bonds.

Until my current one, my job in Lambeth was the longest I held. It was the most busy, fraught and fractious job but fabulous on many levels: in terms of the people I met who were amazing and the amount of things we managed to do and to change! And we got great feedback from people in the community who were using services. Once I got rid of the incompetent staff who were not contributing, it was extraordinary how the creativity of the others burst forth. It was like chopping down weeds in a flower garden. Many of my colleagues came to me to say 'thank you for differentiating between those don't deliver and people who do'. This core of dedicated staff were committed to helping older people and doing three people's jobs to compensate for those who were not doing a damn thing.

The key drivers in my career have always been the mental challenge and achieving recognition. Perhaps if I'd had a family and a mortgage, money would have been a more important motivator!

To young people considering a career in adult social care, I would say: you need to be really clear and realistic about what you can do. I love young people's idealism (which I had myself) but the reality of working in a big bureaucracy like a council can grind you down. You have to balance your idealism with realism. Never stop striving to make things better but accept you may not be able to make things perfect!

I have been sustained during difficult times by many supports from friends, colleagues and family. I was lucky to have a very strong and happy life as a child. My mother died last April, which made me suddenly realise just how important her life long support was. I still have my brother and father.

Also, I am quite analytical and very clear as to what I take responsibility for and what is not my responsibility. I remember a heated discussion with a councillor in Lambeth complaining that I was cutting a particular Age Concern service. I told him that he was responsible at the council for cutting our funding but I was responsible for deciding which of our services to cut back.

And at the end of the day, whatever difficulties I have as a manager, they are nowhere near as hard as those of the people you meet in social care who are in a really tough situation through no fault of their own."

Chapter Thirteen
Particular ASC leadership qualities

Are there particular leadership styles suited to Adult Social Care?

If so, do you possess those qualities, or could you develop them?

Firstly, many of the characteristics of good leaders are shared across all types of organisations and sectors. There are many books on leadership; one that has become very popular amongst top business executives is 'Good To Great' by Jim Collins (*Random House Business, 2011*). The author and his team bring a thorough evidenced-based approach to their analysis of great companies, deploying a very clear objective scale of measurement and assessing the leadership qualities of their chief executives.

A key requirement in their definition of 'great' is sustained high performance. It is not so difficult to achieve excellent results for a short period of time. This can be delivered through a big burst of focused energy or, more cynically, by the manipulation of short-term performance indicators such as the bottom line of a set of accounts or the waiting time for hospital admission. Often the leaders with the biggest egos focus on the shorter

Particular ASC leadership qualities

term and waste no time in trumpeting their achievements, sometimes moving on to a new assignment before the longer-term costs to the organisation become clear.

One of the hallmarks of any truly great leader is a degree of genuine modesty. These leaders tend to ascribe the success of their organisation to luck, good fortune or an excellent staff team. Luck is an interesting concept. There is research evidence that in some sense people with an optimistic outlook on life tend to be 'luckier'. It looks like there is some truth in the old saying 'Fortune favours the brave'. Success in life frequently hangs on your ability to grasp the opportunities that present themselves to you. Sometimes you will not even realise that an apparently insignificant opportunity that someone has offered you could actually be the gateway to something much larger. If an opening feels to you like an opportunity, then don't hesitate – step boldly forward; keep checking if it feels right; if it does, grasp it firmly and run with it as long as it is energising you. And don't be afraid to take a breather – for an hour, a day, or a week – should the energy start to fade.

Another characteristic of a good leader is decisiveness. Yes, a good leader will always listen first. They will be patient with those around them, respecting minority opinions. They will gather information from different sources – including, where possible, from outside their normal circle. They will be well aware that there is always more data, more research, more focus groups that could be arranged, but there comes a point when someone – **you**, if you are that leader – just has to make a decision. As we saw in the chapter on policy, when you are stepping out into an unknowable future you can never be certain what might happen, but if we never dared to take this step then no progress would ever be possible.

This is where faith comes in. Whether you are leading a small group of colleagues, peers or friends, or managing a 1,000-strong organisation, you need to keep faith that you are doing the right thing – for your customers, your staff, your citizens, your shareholders, whoever it might be. This is not quite the same thing as having a Vision, much less does it equate to a Mission Statement. I'm talking here about an inner conviction about the value of your contribution. If appropriate, it may translate into something that you can articulate as a Vision for the group or organisation. Such a vision will motivate all your staff / volunteers / customers, but I'm talking here about what motivates *you*. You don't necessarily need to write this down, but if you do want to articulate it for yourself, then it may help to use pictures and drawings, not just words.

I'm not using the term 'faith' in a religious sense, but it is linked to our core values and beliefs. We all have crises of faith during our lives, when we wonder whether it is all worth the effort of carrying on. When that happens you need to take the time to refer back to what it is that sustains you. For some, that **will** be their religious faith; it might draw on the Bible, the Koran or some other sacred text, or else be nourished by a contemplative visit to the temple, church or synagogue. It may involve paying heed to their priest, vicar or guru: after all, social, or pastoral, care has always been a major part of the priestly role. As I've said before in this book, people in need of social care are often at a personal crisis and as much in need of spiritual support as practical and material assistance.

Other people will find that sustenance in nature, art, in films or literature, in family and friends – even in shopping for a new handbag or planning that purchase of the cool new car (because you're worth it!).

By chance, during the writing of this book, I was invited to join a training course outside Harare on 'The Art of Participatory Leadership', where I met many inspiring young black Zimbabwean civil society activists – positive and enthusiastic despite some of them having suffered wrongful arrest and beatings for their activities. The teachings are sometimes called 'The Art of Hosting', defined as 'an approach to leadership that scales up from the personal to the systemic using personal practice, dialogue, facilitation and the co-creation of innovation to address complex challenges'. (_www.artofhosting.org_)

One of the authors recommended was Dee Hock, founder of VISA, which I discovered was created as and remains a network of member organisations – despite its huge presence globally and the trillions of pounds, dollars, euros, etc transacted through its systems. His book 'One From Many – VISA and the Rise of Chaordic Organization' (Berrett-Koehler, 2005) is well worth a read. To paraphrase, he says that the priorities for a manager come in this order:

1) Manage yourself – your own integrity, character, words and acts. "It is a never-ending, difficult, oft-shunned task. It is ignored precisely because it is incredibly more difficult than prescribing and controlling the behavior of others."

2) Manage your boss (or whoever has authority over you) – without the support of your supervisor, director, regulator, etc, you will not be able to follow your conviction, be creative and achieve constructive results.

3) Manage your peers (those over whom we have no authority and who have no authority over us, including associates, competitors, suppliers, customers) – "Without their respect and confidence, little can be accomplished. Peers can make a small heaven or hell of our life."

4) Manage your staff – and if you think you will have little time left for them after managing the three areas above, then that is exactly right. "Select people of good character, introduce them to the concept, go before and show them how to practice it. If those over whom you have authority properly manage themselves, manage you, manage their peers and replicate the process with those they employ, what is there to do but see they are properly recognized, rewarded and stay out of their way?"

He summarises:

"Lead yourself, lead your superiors, lead your peers, employ good people and free them to do the same. All else is trivia."

These are general rules for leadership. Are there, nevertheless, particular leadership qualities particularly suited to ASC?

Craig Dearden-Phillips gives his angle in his excellent practical book 'How to Step Out – Your guide to leading a mutual or social enterprise spin-out from the public sector' (NESTA, 2011):

"What I like most about the leaders I admire is that their values radiate from them. And not just their service-values either. Their core beliefs and priorities as human beings are very clear from the moment you speak with them. They have integrity. They show care. They are not just task-centred, but people-centred too. They are soft-hearted, but can also be very tough if crossed. But you always know where you are with them."

Let me try and set out the particular qualities, as I see them. I have written in my notes: "A holistic, humanist approach is

Particular ASC leadership qualities

needed". By that I mean that you have to value human beings in their entirety. If you can't feel love towards every human being that you need to engage with (and we can't all be the Dalai Lama!), then try to find them 'a personal challenge' or 'part of the rich fabric' – at the very least, find them interesting. One hears a lot of talk about 'valuing diversity'. Of course, this is usually code for acknowledging and appreciating ethnic, cultural and religious differences but at its heart, for me, is a belief in the shared humanity of us all – at heart we all have similar needs for recognition, family and friends, social interaction, respect, and care. Whatever the cultural differences, these traits were shared by all those encountered by Ewan McGregor and Charlie Boorman as they rode their motorbikes down from John O'Groats to Cape Town, as they describe in their rambunctious account 'Long Way Down' (Sphere, 2008).

Only by being unprejudiced and unbiased will you be able to really connect to the wide range of people you will deal with. (This is not the same as suspending judgement completely.)

Different people have different needs and ways of responding. Patience and understanding provide the key.

A technique currently considered essential in social care policy circles in developing new approaches is 'co-production'. This might best be defined as the process by which 'professionals' and 'service users' collaborate to jointly produce the policy, service or product. Necessarily, the professionals, representing the government or the large organisation such as a big charity, will set the framework within which the project will operate. They will also allocate the resources to be made available, whether these be cash, facilities or their own time. They will also act as the project's champions within the organization, able to navigate its structures in order to achieve the necessary recognition and support.

The 'service users' will bring their own direct experiences to the table. Hopefully, they will offer creative ideas unconstrained by the groupthink of the organisation. Where I have seen this working well, the service users have often cut through some of the cautious, bureaucratic or risk-averse attitudes of professionals. Sometimes it can be a matter of: "just do the little thing X now and don't worry about P, Q & Y for the time being".

On the other hand, to be honest, I often find the concept and practice of 'co-production' problematic. In my experience, there are many, many people who prefer to be led, or at least given some clear options to choose between, rather than being put on the spot to come up with their own ideas. It may just be that they do not have the time or the energy or do not consider the framework posited by the organisation to be a priority for them right now. It takes time and resources for any group of service users to develop the skills and confidence to interact effectively with a more professional organisation. This can be frustrating from the professional's point of view – especially if you have been given a deadline to operate within. In these circumstances, consultation rather than co-production can be more effective. This is about offering a proposals with different options and seeking feedback. You then decide on the degree to which that feedback is taken into account in your final analysis. Sometimes this is a more honest approach.

And that is where one might find the concept of co-production problematic. By definition, it amounts to a compromise between professional leadership and self-organisation by the 'service users'. If one really believes in the predominance, wisdom and abilities of service users, then one would simply allocate them resources, i.e. the project budget, and ask them to get on with it. Occasionally, this has been successful but there is usually a balance which needs to be struck.

Particular ASC leadership qualities

Exercise: Co-Production

As an exercise, take a very small project involving some people in your own immediate life. This could be organising a birthday party or a holiday or perhaps simply deciding what a group of you are going to do next Friday night.

Think about the processes you would normally go through to arrange this.

Write down the different steps.

Now complete that project using the co-production approach.

Set a loose, broad framework – perhaps including an indication of what resources (e.g. money) will be available.

Invite your 'service users' i.e. friends / family / children to come up with ideas, suggestions, proposals for the event.

Make sure you let them shape it.

Insist that they do some of the writing down of the plans – or even the research.

You don't necessarily have to explain why you are doing things differently to what they might be used to.

Follow this through to completion. Make some notes for yourself on the process as it progresses. What is going well, what is surprising you, what is frustrating?

Who amongst your 'service users' is making the strongest contribution? Who is remaining quiet? Is that a problem or might it become one? What enables someone to contribute effectively and why are others quiet?

Afterwards, assess what was more successful as a result of this approach and what was more difficult. If possible, ask the opinions of your 'service users' about both the outcome and the process.

A word of warning: Be careful not to use this with a project that is very important to you and your group and that has a tight timetable. This will be an experiment for you – a different way of doing things, so things may go wrong.

I have focused above on 'co-production' because it is often talked about in the sector, but let me conclude this chapter with some quotations from existing leaders as they discuss their leadership style.

Here's an article by Sherry Malik, Director of Adults' and Children's Services at Hounslow, as published on the Community Care website (*www.communitycare.co.uk*).

"I am nothing without my staff" – leadership lessons from a social services director

Engaging directly with staff, acting with integrity and allowing your opinions to be challenged are among the key lessons that Sherry Malik has learned during her time in social care senior management.

"I am fast approaching the first anniversary of when I

started in my role as director of children and adults in Hounslow and this has led me to reflect on the nature of leadership.

How do you want to 'be' at work?

Before you start the job, think about how you want 'be' at work. How do you want others to perceive you? It's not enough that you know your subject matter and that you have experience. That is a given. This role is about leadership so it is as much about you as a person and your ability to influence, as it is about the authority inherent within the role. I wanted to be a visible leader: approachable, present, being able to connect to my staff and listen to what they wanted and needed in order to be able to do their best every day. This may sound idealistic when you are managing a department with over 1500 staff in multiple locations and there is only one of you.

I had learnt some important lessons in closing the General Social Care Council, the previous regulator for the social work profession, where I was deputy chief executive. Together with Penny Thompson, the chief executive, we embarked on a journey over two years, to keep staff motivated and engaged despite the closure.

Engage with staff on a human level

We learnt how to communicate effectively with not only our staff, but also the wider sector, stakeholders and the 100,000 registrants in England. I learnt the power of social media, blogs, newsletters, visits, speaking at events and answering questions honestly. I learnt the importance of walking the floor, listening to staff and engaging with them at a human level during this two-year period of deep uncertainty. Most importantly I learnt that you can't just do it once but that you need to do it consistently and reliably.

I have actively put this learning to use in Hounslow and visit frontline staff most weeks, walk the floor especially during changes and hold twice-yearly all-staff meetings. On my first Friday I posted a blog for staff, which I have committed to writing every Friday since. (My assistant directors take it in turn when I am on holiday). It is a platform I use to congratulate individuals for their outstanding work, motivate, inform, empathise and get buy in for changes. Colleagues tell me that they look forward to it, not only because it tells them about the work of the department, but because it provides an insight into what the director does, which I am told is often a mystery to many junior staff! I am called by some, affectionately I hope, 'the blog lady'!

Let your values be your guiding light

Leading requires difficult choices and decisions to be made every day and I have always found that when I am facing tough times, my values and principles are my guiding light. Things will go wrong – and there will be many occasions when you will not agree with colleagues on the best way forward. That is without doubt. What matters is how you behave when dealing with these issues – and this is when your values and principles come into play. Work through the problems and issues with integrity, respect, honesty and openness and you can hope to come out of it with your dignity and self-respect intact. You may not always win the arguments, but this isn't about winning, it is about doing the right thing.

Don't let pride get in the way of learning

In the day-to-day challenge of doing the job, I sometimes hear things I don't fully understand – sometimes it is about context and sometimes it is about a particular area of work I am less familiar with. I confess there are times when I wing it, but more often I have taught myself to conquer my pride to ask, 'tell me how this works, 'I don't understand why we do this' or 'what is x?'. This is important because no one can know everything. Pretending that you do doesn't fool any-

one. It only leads to a lack of trust between you and your staff; your opportunity to learn disappears. So don't let pride get in the way of your learning, ask the questions which will ultimately lead to better decision making.

Wilful blindness

I have left this issue to the last deliberately, as it is the most dangerous of mindsets for leaders. Wilful blindness is a legal term used when 'an individual seeks to avoid civil or criminal liability for a wrongful act by intentionally putting him/herself in a position where s/he will be unaware of facts that would render him/her liable' (Wikipedia).

In the case of leaders this translates as being driven by what you believe to be true and right. You then select the information which supports your thinking and choose to ignore information which does not. You choose not to have open debate and discussion about the issues because of fear that you may be proved wrong. But this only drives the debate underground and you lose the pulse.

I have learnt through my mistakes that I am nothing without my staff and that if I allow my opinions to be challenged it is a sign of my strength. I can look back at this past year and see that I have learnt huge amounts not only about the context I work in but also about myself. I know I am aspiring every day to be a better leader."

First published in Community Care (*www.communitycare.co.u*k), 14 August 2013. Reproduced with permission & thanks.

In 2012, I was responsible for managing design and development of the Find Me Good Care website for the Social Care Institute for Excellence (*www.scie.org.uk*). It was a privilege to work with Chief Executive Andrea Sutcliffe, who combines a true humanity with incisive management skills. In October

2013 she took on the highly demanding role of Chief Inspector for Social Care at the Care Quality Commission. This is a critical organization across the whole of the health service as well as social care, responsible for guaranteeing standards of service delivery. Its recent history has been 'troubled', to put it mildly – including cover-ups of its own shortcomings. As Chief Executive since 2012, David Behan will be greatly assisted in putting right previous management shortcomings by having Andrea on his top team.

One of Andrea's skills is making effective use of the media, including tweeting regularly as **@Crouchendtiger7**. On her appointment to CQC she chose to focus on the role of women leaders in social care, but many of her tips apply just as well to men.

Rise of female leaders in social care should be celebrated, says incoming chief inspector

> *"Over the course of my career I have worked in health and social care. In both sectors, the workforce is predominantly female. But it is only in social care where this strength in numbers has translated into prominent female leaders.*
>
> *Just take a look: Annie Hudson and Jo Cleary leading the College of Social Work; Sharon Allen, the chief executive of Skills for Care; Jo again with Debbie Sorkin at the helm of the National Skills Academy for Social Care; Lyn Romeo and Isabelle Trowler appointed as the first chief social workers for England; Sandie Keene this year and Sarah Pickup last*

year as the presidents of the Association of Directors of Adult Social Services; and provider trade associations led by Jane Ashcroft, Sheila Scott, Nadra Ahmed and Jacqueline Bell, among others.

Don't get me wrong. I'm not saying we have completely cracked it in social care, nor that women leaders are better than our valued male colleagues. It just strikes me as an important contrast – and I wonder what that means for female leaders now and in the future in social care.

There is a strong tradition of equal opportunities and valuing diversity in social care and I think this has enabled many gifted women to progress when they might have faced barriers in other sectors.

Of course, we need to ensure that all appointments are made on merit and that anyone taking up a leadership position is capable of doing the job. But women hold only a fraction of leadership roles throughout the working world; those with talent need to be nurtured, supported and developed so they feel confident to put themselves forward for promotion, or for more challenging roles.

Women in leadership positions have a particular responsibility to support and encourage others to follow in their footsteps. We can do this through mentoring and by ensuring that access to learning and development opportunities in our organisations is fair and equitable for all groups. We can also do this by being excellent role models, doing a superb job, demonstrating our values and being ourselves.

We shouldn't fall into the trap of conforming to perceived stereotypes of leaders. We should wear what we want, be human, be open and be approachable. Each of us will need to find our own way to do that. There isn't a one size fits all approach to recommend, but I do have a few tips.

First, don't think you have all the answers. One of the best things I have done in the last 10 years is have an executive coach. That time for reflective practice, with someone whose sole purpose is to help me improve, has been invaluable.

Second, think about your work-life balance. I may not always practice what I preach here, but time for you, your family and friends needs to be cherished.

And my final tip is this: recognise that being a leader is tough. You are in the spotlight. You will have difficult decisions to make and problems to resolve. Finding a coping strategy that works for you is essential.

I focused earlier on women in the most prominent leadership positions, but there are leaders at all levels in social care and lots of them are women. Let's celebrate that and the contribution they make. Let's also ensure we give them the support and encouragement they need to keep the pipeline of talent flowing strong."

First published in Community Care, 2 October 2013. Reproduced with permission & thanks – *www.communitycare.co.uk*

The 'People's Peer'

Lord Victor Adebowale has been Turning Point's Chief Executive since 2001. He was made one of the 'People's Peers' by the Labour Government that same year, after running the youth homelessness charity Centre Point for six years. He was named as one of the top 50 innovators in health services by the Health Service Journal on 6 November 2013. He is a 'cross-bench' peer, which means that he does not 'take the

whip' of any particular party that tells him how to vote. Instead he follows his own conscience.

I interviewed Victor over the phone from a motorway service station on the M4. He was proud of the regional accent in his rich voice which marked him out as a Yorkshireman.

> *"There wasn't really anything in my family or background that influenced me to work with vulnerable people. Except that all my family do 'give a shit'. Just making money is boring. Don't get me wrong, I'm not against making money. It's just that when I look back at the end of my life and ask the question 'Did I leave the world a better place?' I want to be able to say yes. And what matters is people. Much of the world is still a basket case. Some people are luckier than others but most people are in need of something.*
>
> *I have been very lucky. People think I must have sought fame and status but if your motivation in life is fame, then you are doomed. It was a complete and utter accident that I was made a member of the House of Lords. I have been presented with many gift horses in my life and I don't look them in the mouth. I've only ever done the things that make me happy. That has been enough.*
>
> *I started my working life as a volunteer in a housing co-op in Newham. Then I got a job with Patchwork Housing Association. By age 26 I was running an Alcohol Recovery Project.*
>
> *I talked about my early life and time at CentrePoint on Radio 4's Desert Island Discs so you will have to listen to that for the full story. (I'm told it was a privilege to be on there.)*
>
> [You can find it here by entering his name: *http://www.bbc.co.uk/radio4/features/desert-island-discs/find-a-castaway*.]
>
> *You ask me when I realised that I could really 'make a difference'. I'm not sure that I have. It's hard to evaluate. I've*

certainly worked with many organisations that have made a difference. And as a Housing Officer for the council, I helped individuals. The system generally seems to be against helping people, so there has felt an element of subversion. I've sort of campaigned on housing and homelessness and enjoyed that. I'm lucky to work with people including many talented ones in the organisations I've been with.

I've contributed to government policy but, you know, I'd actually be quite concerned if the outcome of policy was the same as planned in theory – because it has to engage with and adapt to real people in real situations.

You talk about rewarding and challenging aspects of a leadership role. Well, guess what? They are different sides of the same coin. At Turning Point I have responsibility for 3,000 staff, 140,000 clients, 250 locations and yes, that's challenging but it's also hugely rewarding. And it's great to have people around me who trust me at times of crisis.

It's rewarding to exercise some little influence in moving the needle of our system in the direction of human beings. I've also been a dustman and swept the roads in my life. **That** *is more challenging than what I do now – especially on an inadequate wage.*

Advice for younger people considering a career in adult social care? It's the same as anywhere: have lots of self-doubt and ambition. If you ever have ambition without self-doubt, then you have the potential to become a sociopath and that's scary. But do allow your ambition to overcome your self-doubt.

The special thing about social care is that you really have to make it a passion because it's hard work.

I would not have done anything different in my career – it's been an incredible learning experience and I don't regret anything.

Particular ASC leadership qualities

> *I'm a six-foot-plus black guy and I know it would have been harder to do what I've done in the 1930s or 50s or even 60s and there is an ever-present challenge. But I've got a fairly strong set of values and think I have a good understanding of what motivates other people. Most people are basically good and want the best for others. Those who are inclined to be more negative usually end up chucking themselves up. I've just made a point of being true to myself and try to treat others as I would wish to be treated."*

"My preferred style is 'trust the frontline staff'."

Julie Boothroyd is Head of Adults at Monmouthshire Council.

> *"It's a bit random, I know, but I became interested in working with older people by accident when I was nineteen years old. My mum ran a hairdressing salon in Huddersfield and lots and lots of older folk came in. I really liked the old ladies. It was a lovely mill town community and I just loved the humour and the fun. The shop was quite a community in itself. We had such characters!*
>
> *Instead of going to university I travelled and worked in France for a while. Then I took a job as a care assistant in a residential home in Bristol. I absolutely loved it from the word go. I liked the older people and working in a team. But interestingly – and it's topical now – it wasn't a particularly good home. Within a few weeks I went to the manager to*

say I was not happy with some of the things that were happening. For example, after lunch they would take people back to the lounge and dump them in the nearest chair to the door without any discussion or choice. It was just wrong. You don't treat people like that.

The management absolutely did listen and a couple of people lost their jobs.

In the mid 80s, I became deputy manager of a joint-funded EMI unit – that stands for 'Elderly Mentally Infirm', a very old term but it was nonetheless ahead of its time. It was a small day centre outreach project for people with early onset dementia, with a few respite beds and some longer-term. We were a young staff team, properly multi-disciplinary, with a consultant, an art therapist, physiotherapist, and a psychologist. We were trying to manage people long-term and at home with the resources we had in the unit. I was seconded to do my CSS social work training from that job – a very good course.

I went on to run a project in Bristol helping younger adults with physical disabilities to become independent. Then I moved to Chepstow in Wales to become an Older Person's Social Worker and was promoted to Senior Social Worker in 1992, becoming team manager for Older People and Physical Disability, amongst other management roles.

I've always made a difference in my work right from my first job and I would not want to do this job without that. A theme running through my career is that we can only really make things better in true partnership with the people who use our services.

At one point I was responsible for transitions from Children's Services. I was getting anxious that we were not getting it quite right and started discussions with colleagues. Then we were approached by three mums who became known as the 'Monmouthshire Mums'. They picked us off one by one, first my Director, then me, and summoned us to a meeting in a pub. Following a discussion I suggested they join our group to help plan the way forward for Transition in Monmouthshire. Honestly, we would not be where we are now without their input. They helped us with transition into adult services for all our young clients – be they ASD, learning difficulty, physical difficulty, looked after children. They led our piece of work very strongly and it went on to win a 'Social Care Accolade' from the Welsh Government.

For me 'making a difference' is learning who it is you can partner, and working with integrity. There are inevitably times when we're not able to meet people's expectations, for example due to insufficient resources.

I suppose what I can bring is the ability to communicate effectively. The modern word is co-production and it's not always an easy path. In Monmouthshire we have a critical mass of good professionals and partners who have been around a long time and know each other very well. Even if the organisations we work for have changed shape and structure over the years, we have maintained relationships, which I think is very key. We are reasonably fortunate in adult services because those changes of organisation and leadership can really disrupt things.

It's always challenging because there is never a lot of money around. So we have a 'make do and mend' attitude, which forces us to be creative. The council has to cut £23 million out of our budget of £126 million over 3 years. For social services that means a seven or eight percent cut. My focus on well-being in the community is necessary but ambitious in that context. It is investing in Local Area Co-ordination and in local networks. It is about how you can better connect people who, yes, have a health problem, but also are essentially lonely.

As a leader my style is lots of styles. Obviously, sometimes you just have to decide and tell. But my preferred style is very much to trust in the frontline staff and, using systems methodology, to remove obstacles for them so they can get on with their work. I have to stay clear on the vision that we have collectively designed together. If people buy into where we're going, then things may be hard, but at least they feel supported. Actually, an important thing I've learned as a leader is that you shouldn't underestimate how important that is.

We are trying to be a networked organisation, as much as you can be in a traditional local authority hierarchy. In the Netherlands they are increasingly taking this approach; a colleague has been over to see some of their social work organisations. We are seeing that old hierarchies are no longer working. They have become wasteful and are no longer adding value. We are also looking how we can 'tip out' some of our functions to a social enterprise or arm's length organisation. I've asked some staff groups to start thinking about what it would mean to no longer be part of a government body. And it's very scary – but very liberating.

Some other councils, such as Carmarthenshire and Caerphilly, are starting to follow our 'systems work' approach to service review. We are about to use the same normative learning approach with our mental health NHS colleagues across five authorities – and they have a very different culture. The systems approach is about getting everyone to understand the system they are in – not plonking a structure on top but seeing what emerges.

I'm sustained by a strong belief in what we are doing and a clear vision, even though it can be really difficult at times. And then I go and ride my horse or go running. And I swear a lot!"

As I conclude this chapter, I'm still not sure I've answered my own opening question. At least, I reckon there's only a partial answer here.

So . . . I suggest you judge for yourself, if you can pick out a common denominator from leaders in ASC that you come across. Some have already been mentioned in this book. You will undoubtedly know others – even if you have not previously considered them 'leaders'. The next chapter will offer some more examples.

You may also be interested, for yourself or your organisation, in what the National Skills Academy for Social Care has to say about leadership under the banner 'Careship':

> *"The ambition of Careship is to educate the entire sector about the need for leadership behaviours, to give them the confidence and knowledge they need to practice them every single day."* (*www.nsasocialcare.co.uk/careship*)

You may also like to check out their test 'Is Social Care for you?' at *www.nsasocialcare.co.uk/training-providers/is-social-care-for-you* – It's aimed at recruits onto a graduate training programme they were running, but may still be of interest.

And, for an international angle, I'd like to end this chapter with some words on Ethical Leadership from Graça Machel.

Making a Difference in Adult Social Care

Graça Machel on Ethical Leadership

Graça Machel is a Mozambican politician and humanitarian. She is the third wife of former South African president Nelson Mandela and the widow of Mozambican president Samora Machel. She is an international advocate for women's and children's rights and in 1997 was made a British dame for her humanitarian work.

She was Minister of Education and Culture in Mozambique 1975-89. With Desmond Tutu, Jimmy Carter, Mary Robinson and others she founded The Elders, a group of world leaders committed to promoting peace and development – see *www.theelders.org*.

Here is what she wrote, on 1 November 2013, to supporters of The Elders:

> *"Dear friends,*
>
> *I am writing to you from Cape Town where my fellow Elders and I have been discussing the meaning of 'ethical leadership' this week during one of our biannual meetings.*
>
> *There is always a moment in your private life, in your organisation, in your community, and in society in general when you ask: what is the right thing to do? A time when you look for a voice to lead and guide you. Someone who has the insight and the wisdom to say the right thing, at the right place, at the right moment, and inspires us to live our*

lives with integrity. More importantly, someone who speaks and resonates with our highest aspirations, and ignites our motivation to live up to our full potential. It is not by chance that when Madiba [Nelson Mandela] founded The Elders in 2007, he turned to Desmond Tutu to lead our group. Archbishop Tutu truly embodies ethical leadership. He speaks truth to power, as well as empowering the disenfranchised, the vulnerable and the marginalised. He is larger than life yet he remains simple and humble, and that is the ethical leadership we wish to emulate. Like him we must stand against injustice, motivated by a compassion that embraces every person and makes every single one feel they matter.

Though Archbishop Tutu has stepped down as Chair and is now an Honorary Elder, we will keep on knocking at his door to ask for guidance on the intractable issues we are bound to tackle. As Elders, we will strive to use our collective clout to bring people together, amplify the space to give voice to the voiceless, and catalyse action. We understand true leadership as that of service, leadership, which promotes equity and dignity for all. Of course, it is not just up to the Elders to define the nature of ethical leadership. What does it mean to you? Who are the ethical leaders that inspire you today? And how can we encourage and foster leaders who put common human values first?"

These questions were at the heart of The Elders' debate in Cape Town televised by the Al Jazeera North2South programme. There is a link at <u>http://theelders.org/article/elders-debate-ethical-leadership-part-1</u>.

Chapter 14

Be inspired by existing leaders

We humans are social animals who learn by observing the behaviour of others and then copying it. In fact, this is true for more or less all animals, to varying degrees. I have just been hearing about birds of prey who 'imprint' their surroundings when they are chicks. This process is so strong that, if they are hand-reared by humans within the first couple of weeks from hatching, then they will associate so firmly with the human 'parent' that they will show absolutely no interest in mating with their own species when they are mature.

So, if you are starting out on your life in the adult social care sector and feel the call to become a leader in some way, then seek out existing leaders to 'imprint' aspects of their behaviour in your mind!

And if this ends up with you only wanting to mate with someone else in the ASC sector, then so be it!

I told you earlier about Terry Dafter's route to becoming a DASS. When he was near the beginning of his career, he was fortunate to work with Jean Daintith, whom he found a very inspiring leader. In his own words, again:

"She was driven, focused and cared passionately about Stockport becoming known as amongst the best performers and somewhere to be proud of."

Be inspired by existing leaders

If he hadn't had the experience of working with her or someone similar, then it is unlikely he would have felt the confidence or motivation to take on the top ASC job in a local authority.

You can make a conscious effort to seek out existing leaders. You probably already know people who play a leading role in their own particular field, even if they may not identify themselves as leaders. Perhaps they are social workers of long standing, ready to share their accumulated experience and wisdom. Or they may have years of running a care home or home care agency under their belt, testimony to their discipline and focus. You might encounter them volunteering in the community, running a support group – or perhaps your own particular hero is an academic with a remarkable record of writing influential and inspiring papers.

Exercise: On Leaders

So, who do you consider might fit this category? It could be someone familiar to you, who has impacted directly on your life, or it might be someone you've never met, but is a source of inspiration to you nonetheless. Take a few minutes and compile a short list, writing down their name – if you know it – and their professional position.

Good! – now here's your homework for the next week: to arrange appointments to go and see at least half of them in the next month. If they are busy, high profile leaders, such as a DASS, maybe you'll be able to catch them speaking at a public meeting.

But, if it's possible, see if you can arrange to meet them one-to-one. Ask them to tell you about their career, about the things that motivated them, what they enjoy, what they might have done differently if they could start over.

If there is one you particularly like, become a groupie!

See if you can spend time working alongside them – whether for an afternoon or for a few months. They might be able to give you some paid work or create a place for you as an intern.

Now, you are not a baby bird; you will already have your own set of values and way of approaching the world. Amongst the ASC leaders that you know, which of them do you particularly respect? Think about their special characteristics. Are these the qualities you would wish to reflect in your own career?

If you get the chance to be around them as they work with other people, notice what it is that makes others pay attention. Is it just what they say or is it how they say it? What role does body language play?

Be inspired by existing leaders

In the meantime, let me give you a few more examples of ASC leaders and their stories.

Birmingham City Council has the largest local authority budget in Europe, with responsibility to a population of more than one million people. Peter Hay is Director of Adult Social Services and has also been President of the Association of DASSs (ADASS). He was a regular consultant during the ministerial discussions on the Health & Social Care Bill and the White Paper on the Long Term Funding of ASC. An example of his co-operative approach is quoted in an 'ADASS Futures' newsletter article:

> Peter was proud to show that Birmingham could contribute by strongly supporting regional activity, and not leading it – despite the overpowering size and wealth that the city brings. He recalls an early meeting of the region where he proposed a joint regional approach to recruitment issues. "There was a stunned silence, then one colleague said: 'we are not used to Birmingham offering to do things with us.'" Thus a new style, and a new approach to regionalism in the West Midlands, was inaugurated.

And don't think you need to have had a university education to reach the top in ASC!

Sharon Allen

Sharon Allen left school with just a few O-levels and is now Chief Executive of Skills for Care, the national employer agency that promotes training and good practice across the ASC sector.

In the words of their website (*www.skillsforcare.org.uk*):

> Skills for Care works with more than 17,000 adult social care employers and other partners to develop the skills, knowledge and values of the 1.5 million workers in our sector.

If you are determined you can have a great career in social care.

Sharon has had an interesting career journey, tackling various hurdles along the way. Here she explains here why you should never listen to your self-limiting beliefs.

> *"One of the barriers to recruiting and retaining people in social care, we are often told, is that there is no career structure. But reflecting on my own career pathway, and those of talented colleagues I've been privileged to work with, I would beg to differ.*
>
> *You might be forgiven for assuming my career started off with a university education – but you'd be wrong. Like many people working in social care, I left school at 16 with a fairly average set of O-levels, and like so many teenagers I had no idea what I wanted to do, but somehow ended up working in a bank.*
>
> *Four roles later and looking for something more fulfilling, I applied for a job as a social work assistant with Derbyshire county council, in its south-east area office. My first piece of career advice is that it is not necessary to have a clear long-term plan about what you want to do – but it is vital to seize every opportunity presented to you with enthusiasm and determination.*
>
> *I quickly came to love my new role, working with people with a learning or physical disability and older people, supporting them where possible to stay in their own homes and supporting them to move into residential care when this was the right option. It wasn't long before my ambition was to qualify as a social worker – but how could I do this? I didn't have any A-levels, let alone a degree.*

However, I learnt not to allow self-limiting beliefs to be the voice I listened to. Make sure you listen to your colleagues, friends, family – everyone and anyone who encourages you to reach out beyond your current experience.

I managed to secure a secondment from my local authority and applied for a course and survived a terrifying interview at Birmingham Polytechnic for the Certificate of Qualification in Social Work. My social work training, both the academic study and the practice placements, taught me so much, and still informs my practice today. Once qualified, I joined Nottingham county council as a community social worker and worked very closely with a great colleague who was a community health worker – integration was up and running even back in the 80s!

Some nine years later, five spent working at a local Women's Aid refuge – which was an amazing, often harrowing, learning experience – I became project manager of an organisation providing services for homeless women and children. This was my first management position, working with a management committee, supervising staff and, because it was a relatively small, voluntary-sector organisation, effectively chief HR, finance and operations manager and sometimes relief project worker when the rota was short.

It was a fantastic learning opportunity, with some seriously scary moments; like when I first looked at the accounts and realised that we had a £20k shortfall, which back then was a lot of money to find. But it's important to face the tough stuff head-on and make the difficult decisions once you've considered all the options.

Seeing for myself the difficulties of rehousing vulnerable people, I decided to complete my professional housing qualification. Three years later, the proud owner of a PG diploma in housing studies and member of the Chartered Institute of Housing, I was offered the opportunity to complete a further

> year's study and obtain that elusive degree. Me, a degree? Yes, finally at the ripe age of 35 I had a degree – so never, ever give up. After six rich and fulfilling years, it was once again time to move on, this time to a national role with Shelter.
>
> Then came my first chief executive role – well, almost – at a well-respected social care and housing organisation. Three weeks into my new role, the founding chief executive, the brilliant Bill Kilgallon, told me he was leaving to go to the Social Care Institute for Excellence. Being appointed chief executive was one of the proudest moments of my career and, when the chance came to lead Skills for Care, I was able to use all I learnt to take up that new challenge.
>
> So, no career pathway in social care? With plenty of determination, the ability to banish any self-limiting beliefs, turn disappointment into opportunity, be courageous and refuse to take no for an answer, I think there are fantastic ways to develop a rewarding career in our sector. The job now is to get that message out there."

Article from Guardian Professional, 4 October 2013

www.theguardian.com/social-care-network/2013/oct/04/social-care-great-career-determined

It is important to see leaders in action – not just read their words. For the next edition of this book, I'd like to offer you video clips!

Find out how leaders came to be in the positions they hold.

Notice not only what has made them effective, but also accept that they are fallible human beings who will sometimes make mistakes. When you get to a position of leadership, this will help you deal with the stresses and not be too harsh on yourself!

Chapter 15

Your Roadmap

Well done, you made it to the final chapter!

(And if you skipped straight here, welcome: you may still get some value from it but you will certainly have more food for thought and, I hope, inspiration if you read the rest of the book!)

I want you to finish with an exercise. I'm asking you to map out your Roadmap to becoming a leader in adult social care. Where will you be able to Make A Difference in Adult Social Care in the future?

You will need to have a little time and space to yourself to complete this last exercise.

This chapter is about thinking into your future, imagining yourself in 2 years' time, in 5 years' time, in 15 years' time. We are always so preoccupied with the present that we rarely get around to doing this. I know that when I was a young man I had no idea of what my future might look like or even what my options were and how I could shape them. I just had a desire to make the world a better place, helping people who were less privileged than myself in their fight for justice, human rights and freedom – and yes, equality. It's a sign of our changing times that the concept of fighting for economic equality almost seems quaint nowadays – despite the academic case recently made so convincingly in 'The Spirit Level'. (Richard Wilkinson & Kate Pickett, *The Spirit Level: Why Equality is Better for Everyone*, Penguin 2010)

Your Roadmap will only be a guide. There are people who say that if you set out on a journey without a clear destination, then you will never arrive. Well, actually, you will arrive somewhere and that place might be a perfectly good location for you – at least for a while. Still, it does help to give your journey some purpose – just be open to new opportunities on the way and keep checking your priorities. I will give you the example of my own gap year travels.

It was way back in 1978, back in the dark days of Soviet State Communism in Eastern Europe, whilst in England the punk scene was just breaking through. I'd met a chef from Romania who had invited me to stay at his hotel and restaurant on the Black Sea, on the condition that I brought with me some English records, which were then impossible to buy in Eastern Europe. Filled with the idealism of youth, I felt inspired by the story of the Russian Revolution, which had overthrown the despotic tsarist regime, and by the stirring promises of communism, so I was up for an adventure behind the 'Iron Curtain' to see for myself what life was like in a supposedly communist country.

I planned my journey carefully. First I accompanied some older friends to their holiday cottage in southern France; then I hitch-hiked across Italy, through Tito's Yugoslavia (in those days still one country), crossing into Romania to reach the Black Sea coast. The journey back was scheduled to be through Hungary and Germany, rendezvousing with my family in Holland before returning to the UK.

It all went pretty much to plan until I tried leaving Romania. My papers were not 'in order' so I was detained for 10 hours and questioned as to where I had stayed and so on. (You know, it was a police state and actually illegal for a Romanian to have a Westerner stay at their house.) When I was allowed to leave, I started hitching from the Romania / Hungary border and met a woman from East Germany who was doing the same.

We got chatting and shared a lift to Budapest. There we shared a tent. Her name was Sylvia and she invited me back to her flat in East Berlin. That was not on my itinerary, but I had fallen a little bit in love, so I accepted. Finding my separate way to Berlin (due to East European visa restrictions) and then having to navigate Checkpoint Charlie several times was an adventure in itself. It was great to stay with Sylvia. She was my first lover and I went back the following New Year (very cold!). I even, as was expected of a Westerner, applied for permission from the communist authorities to marry her. I told them on my application form what a keen student of Marxism-Leninism I was and how I was looking forward to living in East Berlin! In hindsight, I am grateful that my marriage application was refused!!

Nevertheless, I'd had an experience that was enriching, enjoyable and exciting – which, had I stuck strictly to my planned Roadmap, I would never have had. And yet, if I had not planned the trip carefully in advance, I may not have had the confidence to set off at all.

Studying the map

Photo:
Hafiz Ladell

Exercise: Picturing my future

OK, so here is your final exercise.

You'll need three sheets of blank paper – A4 will do, but if you have larger sheets available so much the better. Please find them now before continuing – and have some pencils and crayons handy too.

One sheet will represent where you hope to be in one or two years' time. The next sheet will show where you will be in 5 years' time. The final sheet will indicate how you are really Making A Difference in 15 years' time.

Without taking up too much of your space, write those headings onto the sheets now.

What else are you going to put on each of those pages?

If you have a clear intention for any of those 3 sheets, go ahead and put it down now – either in words or in images.

Carry on with however much is coming to you clearly across the 3 sheets.

If nothing is coming through clearly or when you get stuck, here are some tips and ideas:

* Just pick one sheet to start with – it doesn't matter which one.
* Close your eyes and imagine where you might be at that point in your future. Who will be around you? What will you be doing?
* Your thoughts might not be about your career or adult social care in the first instance – they might be about family or friends or some other aspiration – put these down.
* You may have different options or scenarios come to you – if so, you can divide the sheet into two or three different areas to draw out each of these.
* If words come to you before images, then jot them down.

Your Roadmap

* Try drawing images as well. They don't have to be accurate representations – it's not a drawing competition – as long as they are meaningful to you.

OK – go ahead – get some things down.

Now, I would like you to look back to the first exercise you did in this book. The one where you set yourself a target of Hearts, Stars, Money, Brains.

At the end of this chapter you'll find a whole pageful of these symbols. If you're in a Blue Peter frame of mind I invite you to to get busy with scissors, paste, and coloured pens – colour them in, cut them out and stick them on your sheets, in proportion to the target that you set yourself.

You can distribute the symbols across your three sheets but give particular attention to the 'In 15 Years' Time' page.

Also, particularly for that '15 Years' sheet, think about aspects outside of your ASC career. Do you expect to have started (or expanded) your own family by then? If you were actually planning the detailed route and timetable for that destination, then you should also allow time for contingencies – perhaps a problem with your career outside of your control (such as public sector spending cuts and redundancies!) or a relative becoming ill and needing care. However, you don't need to worry about that at the moment.

For the '15 Years' sheet think back to the different chapters and leadership roles that were described. Which appealed to you? Which can you see yourself doing? E.g.:

* Senior manager in an Adult Social Services Department?
* Running a care home or a home care agency?
* Managing a Social Enterprise?
* Working in a charity?

- ✳ Being a well-respected and quietly inspiring individual amongst your peers in your workplace or your community?
- ✳ Being a politician focusing on ASC locally or nationally?
- ✳ Speaking and writing and researching on ASC policy, in England, the UK, Europe or globally?

OK, off you go. Finish those 3 sheets now.

And finally, I hope that this book has given you some ideas that you had not considered. Perhaps it has inspired you to explore different career options and to set yourself some ambitious targets.

If you have read through the book to the end, then something is pulling you towards Making A Difference in Adult Social Care. There may also be factors in society that are pushing you towards working in that field. These may be expressed by advice from parents, teachers, friends or just the promise of being able to earn a living.

Either way, where you can find alignment between that pull inside of you and the push of society, there you will be able to find harmony and happiness and make a real contribution. Go for it, girls and boys!

And good luck!

Richard Pantlin, Oxford 2014

Acknowledgements

Many people have helped make this book possible. The spark came from reading Daniel Priestley's inspiring book 'Become a Key Person of Influence' (Ecademy Press, 2010). This directed me to Mindy Gibbins-Klein, whose residential course gave me the courage to find my own voice and identify my audience. I thank my 'Book Midwife' buddies from that course for their encouragement: Maria Adebowale and Lotwina Farodoye. In the drive towards completion my old friend Hafiz Ladell has been absolutely invaluable, harnessing his various passions – for semi-colons, capitalisation, dingbats – into the combined role of copyeditor, proofreader and layout artist.

Reviewers of my first full draft gave very helpful feedback: Sophie Kendall, Lorna Wallace-Davis, Tony Brockman, Sonya Welch-Moring and Sophie Dishman.

The book would not have happened had I not taken the leap from the secure corporate world into freelance consultancy back in 2011. Tony Barron was key in giving me the courage to do so and arranged my first contract – thank you!

Contributors of their personal stories gave up their valuable time and are acknowledged in the text – as are authors of referenced books, articles, illustrations. Particular gratitude goes to Fran Orford for his wry and witty cartoons which offset my own natural optimism.

I thank Alexandra Lewis, my 'second wife' and mother of my beautiful younger son, for her patience, indulgence and support during the book's gestation. My daughter, Yasmin Spark, contributed an excellent, speedy final proofread, and her enthusiasm for the content has encouraged me to put the work out into the world.

Any inaccuracies or omissions are, of course, entirely my own responsibility.

Page for making notes

Page for making notes

Bibliography

Blond, Phillip, *Red Tory*, Faber & Faber, London, 2010

Brooks, David, *The Social Animal – a story of how success happens*, Short Books Ltd, London, 2nd revised edition 2012

Collins, Jim, *Good To Great*, Random House Business, London, 2011

Dearden-Phillips, Craig, *How to Step Out – Your guide to leading a mutual or social enterprise spin-out from the public sector*, NESTA, London, 2011

Dilnot, Andrew, et al, *Fairer Care Funding: The Report of the Commission on Funding Care and Support (The Dilnot Report)*, Department of Health, 2011

Hock, Dee, One From Many: VISA and the Rise of Chaordic Organization, Berrett-Koehler, San Francisco, 2005

Institute of Public Care, *Report*, Oxford Brookes University, 2010

McGregor, Ewan and Boorman, Charlie, *Long Way Down*, Sphere, London, 2007

Norman, Jesse, *The Big Society: the Anatomy of the New Politics*, The University of Buckingham Press, Buckingham, 2010.

Peter, Laurence J & Hull, Raymond, *The Peter Principle: Why things always go wrong*, William Morrow and Company, New York, 1969

Putting People First Consortium, *People Who Pay for Care*, Oxford Brookes University, 2011

Wilkinson, Richard & Pickett, Kate, *The Spirit Level: Why Equality is Better for Everyone*, Penguin, London, 2010

Websites referred to in the text

www.adass.org.uk
www.artofhosting.org
www.basw.co.uk British Association of Social Workers
www.bbc.co.uk/radio4/features/desert-island-discs/find-a-castaway
www.breakbarrierscic.com
www.carers.org.uk
www.communitycare.co.uk
www.communitycatalysts.co.uk/
www.theelders.org
www.findmegoodcare.co.uk
www.funzimride.co.uk
www.theguardian.com/social-care-network/
www.hpc-uk.org The Health and Care Professions Council
https://mqi.ic.nhs.uk/ NHS Information Centre
www.nsasocialcare.co.uk/careship National Skills Academy for Social Care
www.nottinghamshire.gov.uk
www.pureinnovations.co.uk/
www.salvere.co.uk/
www.schoolofmovementmedicine.com
www.scie.org.uk The Social Care Institute for Excellence
www.scope.org.uk
www.skillsforcare.org.uk
www.takingcontroloxon.org.uk/pa
www.tcsw.org.uk The College of Social Work
www.worksmart.org.uk

Index

Adebowale, Victor, 196-9
Age Concern, 48, 181
Age UK, 25, 43, 48, 65, 97, 99, 128, 152, 153-5
Allen, Sharon, 209-12
Askwith, Shirley and Nelson, 138-9
Barbour, Meg, 21, 23, 48, 86-95, 126, 161
Behan, David, 58, 113, 170, 194
Bolton, John, 113
Boothroyd, Julie, 199-202
Break Barriers Ltd, 64, 135-7
Buckley, Charlotte, 172-176
Bureaucracy, 122-3
Burstow, Paul, 57
Cann, Paul, 153-5
Cartoons by Fran Orford, 27, 30, 48, 121, 122, 133, 164, 186, 219
CIC (Community Interest Company), 64, 137, 145, 146, 150, 151
Community Care online magazine, 45, 47, 99, 190, 193, 196
Community Care Act 1990, 82, 109,
Community Catalysts, 151
Co-production, 187-9
CQC (Care Quality Commission), 59, 136, 194
Dafter, Terry, 14-15, 104-5, 115-6, 121, 206
Dementia, 86, 95, 146, 147, 200, 224
Dementia, worldwide cost, 43
DH (Department of Health), 53-4, 58, 62, 98, 113, 169, 171, 172, 174
Dilnot Report, 42, 45
Douglas, Anthony, 112
ECCA (English Community Care Association), 177
Find Me Good Care, 62, 193
FunZimRide, 36-7
Gilroy, Peter, 112
Greaves, Sue, 128-9
Green, Martin, 177-81
Hay, Peter, 106, 111, 117, 140, 209
Jerome, Jeff, 113

Killeen-Mcguirk, Nessa, 127
Kramer, Richard, 158, 159-60
Lake, Robert, 113
Lamb, Norman, 55
Lansley, Andrew, 55-7
Lewis-Longwe, Andrene, 135-7
Machel, Graça , 204-5
Malik, Sherry, 190-3
Mason, Glen, 113
Monopoly, 142
User-Led Organisations (ULOs), 98, 158
Maslow hierarchy of needs, 83
Monmouthshire Council, 199
NICE (National Institute for Clinical Excellence), 60
National Skills Academy for Social Care, vi, 194, 203
Nottinghamshire CC, 117
Pearson, David, 117-8
Personalisation, 19, 20, 58, 82, 110, 115, 124, 157, 162, 169
PACT (Prison Advice and Care Trust), 127
Pure Innovations, 147
Ross, Julia, 113
Rowse, Janet, 147-8
Salvere, 148
SCIE (The Social Care Institute for Excellence), 193, 212, 224
Sense, 159-60
Sirona, 147
Skills for Care, vi, 44, 194, 209-10, 212
Sloss, Stephen, 113, 148-50
Social worker jobs and pay, 47
Soldiers' and Sailors' Families Association, 129
Sorkin, Debbie, 196
Spending on social care, 42
Stott, Martin, 71-5
Sutcliffe, Andrea, 193
Templeton, Robert, 129-30
Turning Point, 152, 158-60, 196, 198

About the author

Richard Pantlin is a leading independent expert on English Adult Social Care systems. He advises the government on the information system implications of policy changes.

In September 2013 the Association of Directors of Adult Social Services (ADASS) published his report on the government's care funding reforms: 'Implementing Dilnot: just more data or a driver for change?' He continues to work with ADASS, helping councils prepare for the Care and Support Act and for a more integrated collaboration with the NHS.

In 2012 Richard managed the design and development of 'FindMeGoodCare.co.uk' for the Social Care Institute for Excellence (SCIE). He also developed a service, with the Oxford Health Foundation Trust and Neighbourhood Watch, for volunteers to help find people with dementia who go missing.

He previously had various management roles in commercial companies supplying the social care and local government sector.

Richard offers his own style of one-to-one coaching and support to leaders in the health & social care sector – 'CareStellations' – applying the powerful methodology of systemic constellations to organisations. See *www.richardpantlin.com* for more details.

He is also founder of Socially Enterprising Services Ltd.